ROSÉ

by JEFF MORGAN

photographs by FRANCE RUFFENACH

A GUIDE TO THE WORLD'S MOST VERSATILE WINE

ROSÉ

CHRONICLE BOOKS

SAN FRANCISCO

Text copyright © 2005 by Jeff Morgan.

Photographs copyright © 2005 by France Ruffenach.

Library of Congress Cataloging-in-Publication Data available.

ISBN 0-8118-4355-6

Manufactured in Hong Kong.

Designed by Warmbo Design
Food Styling - Amy Nathan
Food Styling Assistant - Katie Christ
Prop Stylist - Sara Slavin
Typesetting by Warmbo Design

The photographer wishes to thank Amy Nathan for beautiful food,
Sara Slavin for impeccable style, Katie Christ and Cedric Glasier
for their tireless support, Jeff Morgan for inspiring content and
Aya Akazawa for her spirited enthusiasm.

Distributed in Canada by Raincoast Books
9050 Shaughnessy Street
Vancouver, British Columbia V6P 6E5

10 9 8 7 6 5 4 3 2 1

Chronicle Books LLC
85 Second Street
San Francisco, California 94105

www.chroniclebooks.com

acknowledgments

This book could not have been written without a lot of help from my friends and colleagues throughout the wine world. My biggest supporter and inspiration is Daniel Moore, who keeps SoloRosa on an even keel and who has worked with me since the very beginning in our quest to make fine rosé.

My New York wine guru, Larry Perrine, got me started with barrel-fermented rosé on Long Island when we were both much younger. Additional thanks stateside go to Californians Dawnine Dyer, Lori Griffin and her rosé avengers, the staff at Swirl, Dan Fredman, Elias Karkabasis, Jeff Gargiulo, Mat Garretson, Paige Poulos, Anthony Terlato, Pete Danko, Kristina Corelli, Carol Shelton, Mitch Mackenzie, and my West Coast wine guru, David Ramey. Steve Burns offered insights from Washington state.

Overseas, Charles, Philippe, and Zara Bieler were all instrumental in giving me a proper introduction to the world of French rosés. Olivier and Emmanuelle Ott, Paul and Laurent Bunan, Jean-Louis Carbonnier, Martine Saunier, Kermit Lynch, Hiram Simon, Kurt Eckert, Philippe Kessler, François Millo, Gilles Masson, and Richard James were equally helpful in showing me the road to discovery in France. Matthew Fioretti, Brian Larky, and Glen Salva helped me navigate Italy. From Down Under, Rob McDonald and Max Allen provided invaluable assistance.

Rosé is best with a good meal. Chefs Lars Kronmark of the Culinary Institute of America's Napa Valley campus; Michael Reardon of Tra Vigne, also in Napa Valley; and Terry Stark of Willi's Wine Bar in Sonoma County all shared their expertise and good taste.

Of course the bottom line resides with my editors, Bill LeBlond and Amy Treadwell, who set the ball in motion and gave me a tremendous opportunity to share what I know while also expanding my own horizons. Copy editor Carrie Bradley ensured clarity and correctness. France Ruffenach made everything look beautiful.

Finally, thank you Jodie, Skye, and Zoë, for putting up with my constant and daily swirling, sipping, spitting, note taking, muttering, and raving. I couldn't make it without you.

—JM

TABLE OF CONTENTS

introduction

Not long ago, diners at America's best restaurants would have been hard-pressed to find rosé—French or American—on the wine list. It was considered unworthy in the United States, despite the fact that rosé is the most widely produced wine in much of southern France—where good living and eating are time-honored traditions.

The greatest challenge to rosé's rightful place at the American table is the perception that pink wine is inherently sweet—a kind of wine soda pop. That's because a number of sweet, pink wines—mostly from Portugal and California—have enjoyed enormous commercial success in the United States. Their prominence has overshadowed the many fine rosés that are fermented dry or unsweetened.

There also seems to be an odd male aversion to rosé. Apparently the color pink presents a stereotypical stigma in the eyes of certain men—particularly in the New World. As a result, they have eschewed drinking pink in public. It's too bad. They're missing out on one of the world's most satisfying and versatile wines.

Fortunately, times and tastes are changing. Today, rosé has become de rigueur among food cognoscenti and bon vivants alike. Dry rosé now graces the wine lists of many fine restaurants, and wineries from both the Old and New World are increasing their production to satisfy consumer demand.

Like its red and white wine cousins, rosé comes in many styles. Tradition, climate, and wine-making techniques vary from region to region and from winery to winery. The result is a richly diverse array of pink wines from which to choose.

This book seeks to capture the personality of rosé through its history, geography, and culture. Newcomers to the category will hopefully discover another realm of wine enjoyment. Rosé aficionados should also find information to help them expand their understanding and appreciation of the genre. At the heart of this study lies a confluence of elements based on universal standards of good taste and good living.

1 what is rosé?

In French, *rose* means pink. As in English, the word also refers to the premier flower of romance. But when that little accent is added to the last letter, *rosé* takes on added significance—the name of one of the world's most versatile wines.

Lacking a true rosé wine tradition, we Anglophones have adopted the French word to describe pink wine. After all, the French are clearly the leaders in the category—at least in terms of volume made and consumed. But other countries, such as Spain and Italy, have wine of the same hue and their own words for it. The Spanish drink *rosado*, while the Italians say *rosato*; in Germany, they call it *Weissherbst*.

why is it pink?

Like red wine, rosé takes its color from the skins of red grapes. Intensity of color will vary, depending on the grape varieties used and the length of time the skins remain in contact with the juice. This duration varies from less than an hour to as long as several days or more. Extended skin contact will yield a wine almost red in color, while a very short maceration period may produce a wine that is nearly—but not quite—white. There are rosés that are made simply by blending red and white wine, but many of the best rosés (with the exception of sparkling) are produced by means of a method known as *saignée* (pronounced "sen-yay"), a French word that means "to bleed." The concept may not sound particularly appetizing, but it does follow a certain logic. After a short maceration time, the pink colored juice is "bled" out of the fermentation tank and thus separated from the grape skins.

To begin the process, at harvest, red grapes are picked and brought to the winery to be destemmed and crushed. The stems are discarded, and the skins and juice are pumped into a tank. Through this stage, the winemaking process is identical for both red and pink wines.

Within a few hours, the grape skins begin to separate from the juice. They rise to the top of the tank, where they create a "cap" of skins. To increase color intensity, red wine makers must regularly re-submerge the cap into the juice.

But rosé producers don't want their pink wines to turn red. So before that occurs, they separate the juice from the skins. Once the cap has formed, a valve at the bottom of the tank is opened, and the pink colored juice can be pumped, or "bled," off into barrels or tanks to ferment. Some English-speaking winemakers refer to the *saignée* method as "cap and drain."

After this stage, the rosé process is more akin to making white wine, which is fermented with little or no skin contact. Whether fermented in barrels or tanks, the wine is allowed to "go dry," which means that all of the natural grape sugars are consumed by fermenting yeasts.

The *saignée* method may also be used by winemakers to increase intensity in their red wines. In this case, only a small portion of juice is bled away from the skins to make rosé. But the remaining juice stays in contact with the skins. Because there is a greater surface area ratio of skins to juice after the bleed, more color (and possibly complexity) can be extracted from the skins into the red wine-to-be.

As a result, some people refer to rosé made by the *saignée* process as a byproduct of red wine production. Technically, they're right, but in this instance the concept of a secondary product should not be viewed in a derogatory sense. The so-called byproduct is, in fact, beautiful free-run juice that produces some of the best rosés on the planet.

Some top rosé producers, particularly in the south of France, prefer not to "bleed" their grape juice. Instead, they treat red grapes destined for rosé much as they would grapes for a white wine. After the grapes are harvested, they are crushed and quickly pressed or whole cluster pressed—just as white wine grapes are—directly into a fermenter. In this way, there is little or no skin maceration. Not surprisingly, wines made in this fashion are a lighter shade of pink.

the grapes

European winemakers typically make rosé from the red grape varieties traditionally grown in their home regions. Some white grapes may also find their way into the blend for added complexity.

In southern France, red grapes such as Grenache, Mourvèdre, Cinsaut, and Carignan are commonly used exclusively or in a blended fashion. In other areas of the country, such as the Loire Valley to the north, Pinot Noir or Cabernet Franc may become the core variety. In Italy, Sangiovese may serve as a point of departure, and in Spain, it may be Tempranillo or Cabernet Sauvignon. Basically, any red grape can be used for making pink wine. Rosé is not a varietal, but rather a category of wine.

New World winemakers typically have fewer varietal constraints or preconceptions than their Old World counterparts. Tradition in the New World is a fairly fluid concept. In California, it's not uncommon to find rosé made with Grenache, Cabernet Sauvignon, Cabernet Franc, Merlot, Sangiovese, Syrah, Pinot Noir, and, of course, Zinfandel—either as single varietals or blended. Any of these red grapes can produce fine pink wine.

As with any wine, the chosen grape variety affects the flavor and style of a rosé. Grapes such as Merlot and Syrah have different flavors, which can become even more pronounced when these varieties are grown in diverse climates and soils. Warmer regions tend to produce more full-bodied rosés, while cooler areas typically make leaner, brighter, and lighter-bodied wines.

Nonetheless, varietal distinction may not be as significant for rosé as it is for red wines made from the same grapes. Reduced skin contact prior to or during fermentation produces somewhat blurred differences among the red varietals.

In some regards, the rules for red don't apply to rosé. My experience leads me to believe that the key to rosé wine quality is less dependent upon the given varietal than upon the maturity of the grapes. Ultra-ripe grapes typically produce a more full-bodied, fruity wine, while less ripe grapes produce a brighter textured, lighter, and more understated wine. Ripeness is most consistently a reflection of regional provenance, so while you may prefer Syrah to Sangiovese in red wines, you might well have a completely different perspective for pink wine.

fermentation

For all wines, yeast processes the natural grape sugars in grape juice to create alcohol. Yeasts are found throughout nature—and that includes on grape skins. These yeasts (similar to those that make bread rise) can spontaneously begin fermentation in freshly crushed grapes. When this occurs, winemakers call it a native, or indigenous, yeast fermentation.

However, many winemakers prefer to use commercially developed yeast strains that are designed to bring out particular characteristics in a wine. Some of these yeast are known to create a fruitier style, while others might tone down fruitiness. It's a question of choice that reflects a winemaker's vision for both the winemaking process and the finished product.

Sometimes the yeast don't finish processing all the sugar in a fermenting wine, which can leave varying traces of sweetness that are often not apparent to the average taster. In minute quantities, this residual sugar can enhance the perception of fruitiness in a wine. Alternatively, a winemaker may boost sweetness by adding grape juice concentrate. The latter practice is not typical for high-quality rosé.

wood versus steel

Choosing whether to ferment a wine in small barrels or large tanks is an important decision for makers of rosé, as with other wines. Stainless-steel or concrete tank fermentation

SHADES OF PINK

Winemakers and wine drinkers alike may become concerned if their rosé seems too light in color; a lighter shade of pink perhaps suggests that the wine is somehow less "serious," or will be less flavorful. In truth, however, there are many shades of excellence in rosé.

Rosé's color comes from grape skins; so do the astringent tannins that give certain red wines a drying effect on the palate. Yet rosé should be as smooth textured as a white wine, which is made with little or no skin contact. A very dark rosé may have had extensive skin contact and so may also be somewhat astringent. Other dark rosés have simply been produced with grapes high in color compounds, which quickly leach into the juice. Still others have been made with very ripe grapes that have smooth, supple tannins anyway. So don't rule out dark pink wines; they can be quite elegant.

By the same token, don't dismiss a light-colored rosé as being wimpy. It may be bursting with flavor, just like your favorite Chardonnay or Sauvignon Blanc—both white wines. Some regions, like France's Sancerre and Côtes de Provence, typically produce light-colored wines. Some are incredibly intense and others are not.

Try not to get bogged down on the question of color. Old, tired rosés can indeed take on an orange veneer that comes from oxidation, and should be avoided. But in general, look for pink wines based on a recommendation or your own experience. Wine is for drinking—not looking at. So let your palate—and not your eyes—be the judge of quality.

highlights fruit flavors and gives a rosé a lighter feel on the palate. It's a commonly used technique that can yield remarkably fresh and lively wines of distinction.

By contrast, some winemakers prefer to ferment their rosés in oak barrels. This is called an "oxidative" approach, because a certain amount of air passes into the wine through the barrel staves. The resulting wine may have a rounder, richer mouth feel than it would have had if fermented in a stainless-steel tank. With barrel fermentation, fruitiness may be toned down as well. As a rule, older, "neutral" barrels are used to prevent the delicate qualities of the wine from being overwhelmed by the oaky flavors found in newer barrels. Sometimes rosé is made from a blend of tank-fermented and barrel-fermented wine in an effort to harvest the best of both styles.

drinking pink

- A QUESTION OF STYLE

When we talk of "style" in a wine, we're actually invoking a pretty simple concept. Is your rosé dry or sweet? Is it full-bodied or lighter on the palate? Perhaps it has a creamy, smooth texture. Or maybe it's tangy and bright, or a little of both. These are all stylistic considerations.

Differences in style are what make wines interesting. If every rosé tasted alike, drinking pink would quickly become a dreary prospect. So when the pundits say that all rosé should be fresh and light on the palate, it's an unfortunate simplification. Like most white wines, rosé benefits from good acidity, which gives a measure of freshness and firmness. But the difference that exists between a bracing, citrusy rosé from Sancerre, France, and a lush, almost jammy Australian rosé is enormous. Rosé may be full-bodied, medium-bodied, or light-bodied; fruity and broad on the palate or bone-dry, crisp, and mineral-like.

A wine's style derives from both the vineyard and the way it is made. In cooler climates like those typically found in France, grapes retain higher acidity and lower levels of sugar. Less sugar means that the fermenting yeast will have less food to eat, and therefore will produce a wine lower in alcohol. Since alcohol has weight, we think of low-alcohol wines as light-bodied. Heightened acidity and light body can translate to a zippier, fresher mouth feel that sometimes carries mineral overtones as well.

In warmer regions, such as California, riper grapes yield more sugar, lower acidity, and more vivid fruit flavors. As a result, warm-climate rosés tend to be more full-bodied, creamier on the palate, and fruit-driven, even when made in a bone-dry style.

Of course, these generalizations are riddled with exceptions. Because of subtle variations in climate and widely varied cellar techniques, winemakers the world over are producing a startlingly diverse array of rosés.

What's most important to understanding rosé is that it is not a narrow wine category bound in a shallow, one-word descriptor. The many and varied hues of rosé carry equally varied qualities ranging from lush, round, full, fruity, complex, and broad to lean, steely, bright, austere, fresh, and firm. There is no "correct" or even "typical" style of rosé; by tasting, you will discover your own preferences.

• NOT JUST FOR SUMMER

Yes, there is that refreshingly bright, cool, light rosé made for a warm summer afternoon, perfectly suited to wash down a dozen oysters on the half shell. But there are also many full-on, robust rosés styled for a cooler evening and featuring richer fare, such as Pork Tenderloin with Ancho Chile Sauce (page 98).

It's only logical that we drink more chilled white or pink wines in the summer than we do in the winter. Yet we don't stop drinking white wines when the weather turns cool; I'm not ready to tuck into a plate of raw shellfish accompanied by a rich, full red wine. But a crisp rosé enhances seafood and many other kinds of dishes in the winter as well as the summer.

• WINE TEMPERATURE

Rosé is best drunk chilled. Like a white wine, it is blessed with the kind of firm acidity most appreciated at a cool serving temperature.

How cold is "cool"? That depends. On a searingly hot summer day, throngs of French diners on the Côte d'Azur can be observed at their beachside cafés downing copious amounts of rosé over ice. Of course, watering down your wine with melting ice hardly enhances its finer points, but rosé on the rocks can be the perfect refreshing luncheon drink, and sometimes that's what counts most. When I'm feeling particularly parched, I also like to top off a glass of cool, chilled bubbly water with a splash of rosé. The bubbles seem to carry all the flavors of the wine in a delicious way, while you enjoy an *almost* nonalcoholic quaff.

A well-made rosé will benefit from the same treatment you would accord an equally fine white wine. That said, any wine served too cold will be hard to taste, and that includes most wines as they emerge from the refrigerator. Within 10 minutes at room temperature, a chilled rosé will probably be drinking best. And assuming you are not dining in tropical heat, a bottle of rosé should taste just fine as it warms up somewhat during the course of your meal.

I keep a refrigerated bottle of wine cool while dining by placing it in an insulated, clear plastic wine cooler. The cooler doesn't actively chill the wine, but simply prevents it from warming up too fast. And because the plastic is transparent, the bottle and label are still visible.

A typical ice bucket tends to make a wine too cold. But if that's all you've got to chill down a warm bottle, then use it. Just remember to remove your bottle from the ice for a while now and then. It's a bit of a juggling act, but worth it.

• GLASSWARE

The shape and size of a wineglass does indeed make a difference in enjoying wine. Much of what we taste is really what we smell. That means that at least half the volume of your wineglass should be dedicated to collecting aroma—not liquid. If possible, use a wineglass no smaller than 10 ounces, but fill it only one-third to one-half of the volume with wine. The empty area will collect the aromas that rise naturally out of wine and direct them to your nose, which should be placed squarely inside your glass.

By no means a snobby ritual, this method lets you smell, and therefore taste, the wine better. Swirl your glass a bit and the aromas will become even more apparent. Sniff, swirl, and then take a sip. This isn't something you need to do with any religious regularity before each sip, but it's a nice way to get to know your wine. I like a glass that's thin lipped, without a wide edge to the rim. This seems to allow the wine to make a smoother transition to your palate.

In terms of price, you can spend a lot on a good wineglass. Austrian-based Riedel is perhaps the most famous wineglass maker, and indeed, the company makes a wide array of excellent glasses, many of which are quite pricey, and well worth it. Riedel also makes several lines of less expensive glasses that are eminently suitable for nearly any table and any wine. Spiegelau, recently purchased by Riedel, is another fine producer of wineglasses, and generally less expensive, too. Beyond these recommendations, just keep the guidelines of 10 ounces and thin-lipped edges in mind, and you'll surely find a fine glass for your wine.

A note on picnics, a favorite venue for rosés: bring paper cups, rather than plastic, if you can. But I'll drink any good wine out of a plastic cup if that's all there is available.

ROSÉ AND AGEING

Most rosé is meant to be drunk young, when its flavors are vivid and fresh. But some rosés have more staying power than others. Those with bigger, bolder character will retain their appeal longer than lighter, ephemeral wines.

This was vividly illustrated to me during a visit to Tavel, a southern French appellation—or wine-growing region—dedicated exclusively to rosé. Franck Popek, who makes wine at Canto Perdrix, foraged about in his cellar and found a bottle of 1954 rosé tucked away. He opened it and poured the forty-nine-year-old, golden-hued liquid into our glasses. It had lost its pink color, but retained an extraordinary amount of flavor, redolent of truffles and honey in the nose. On the palate, it was still very much alive, showing bright acidity and a firm focus. Hints of apricots, tart apples, more honey, and grapefruit flavors tickled the tongue in a long embrace. It was a stunning wine and a surprising revelation.

Nevertheless, approach rosés that have more than two or three years in the bottle with some caution. For some unknown reason, that 1954 Tavel held onto its vitality long after most wines—red, white, or pink—would have given it up. Most of today's rosés are simply not made for the cellar.

If you find an older vintage in a wineshop or on a wine list, ask the merchant or sommelier if he or she has had the wine lately. If not, consider purchasing a younger wine.

Of course, there is no substitute for tasting a wine yourself. In a restaurant, that shouldn't be a problem. However, wineshops are hampered by varying state laws that may forbid tastings on-site. So you might have to buy an older bottle on faith alone. A good wine merchant will taste inventory that's particularly time sensitive and should be able to describe the drinkability of an older rosé. When in doubt, always ask.

The exception to the rule of older pink wines is sparkling rosé, which—like other sparkling wines—can age beautifully over many years. Color may decrease dramatically, but the flavors remain and evolve in the bottle. Remember, however, that sparkling rosé should be stored in a cool environment with minimum temperature variation, in the same manner as white or red collectibles.

WHAT'S IN A NAME: ROSÉ, BLUSH, OR JUST PINK WINE?

Pink wine can take on many hues. Some are barely pink—almost clear, like a white wine. Others are darker hued, and might even be confused with light red wine. Most fall somewhere in between.

The French, who make more pink wine than anyone else, call it *rosé*. Maybe that's why this is the most commonly used moniker. Sometimes the French use the term *vin gris*—literally "gray wine"—for a light colored rosé.

The Italians call it *rosato*, and the Spanish say *rosado*. The German descriptor is *Weissherbst*. "Blush" is a phrase commonly used in the New World, especially America, where it often describes a sweeter style of rosé. But blush can also refer to a drier wine style, depending on who's talking.

In deference to the French and most wine drinkers throughout the world, I usually use the term *rosé*. "Blush" doesn't really appeal to me, as it also implies that symptom of emotional discomfort in our faces. "Pink wine" works just fine for the category, but it doesn't seem to roll off the tongue with quite the same aplomb as *rosé*.

White Zinfandel, nearly always made in a sweet style, should not be confused with dry rosé. (Dry rosé can be made from Zinfandel grapes, however.) Although White Zin is actually pink, the word "white" was initially created for the title of this newly developed wine as a marketing tool to attract white wine drinkers to what was better known as a red varietal. For more about this California phenomenon, see page 48.

In the end, you can call rosé whatever you like. There's plenty of meaning in a name, but it's nothing compared to what's in the bottle.

2 | france:
A UNIQUE CULTURE
OF ROSÉ

In the French town of Aix-en-Provence, you can drive from the picturesque old city's center to its less-charming industrial and suburban outskirts in about ten minutes. Here you'll find shopping malls with gargantuan grocery stores like Carrefour, which offer good values and great quantities of both wine and food.

The mammoth-sized wine department at Carrefour features a seemingly endless display of wines. But what shocked me most was the extraordinary number of rosés on display. I counted more than two hundred fifty different labels one cold November afternoon, while the aisles were bustling with customers searching for their favorite producers.

In Provence, they apparently drink rosé year-round, in both hot and cold weather.

"If you go to a different supermarket, you'll probably find another two hundred fifty different rosés," said Hélène Roux, a salesperson at the store. "Every winery in the region makes rosé, and because we have so many wineries here, we have a large number of rosés to choose from."

Indeed, in the Côtes de Provence wine region, some 85 percent of the wines made are rosés. In nearby Bandol, which is south of the port town of Marseille, rosé is also king, although red and white wines are produced there as well. Perhaps most striking, in terms of a dedication to pink wine, is the town of Tavel, to the north, near Châteauneuf-du-Pape. Tavel has taken the high road by defining itself exclusively with rosé. Virtually all the grapes grown there are made into pink wine.

You'll find rosé made in just about every wine region in France. In the Loire Valley, a number of different styles are made. In Champagne, sparkling rosés are among the most highly regarded and most expensive wines produced (see page 59). Burgundy's small production comes from the Marsannay district. And in Bordeaux, where *rouge* is de rigueur, locals call their rosés by the name *clairet*. In fact, nearly everyone who makes red wine in France makes a little rosé on the side, even if not for sale commercially.

But only in Provence, at the southern end of the country, does there exist a true culture of rosé. In Provence, rosé is considered a principal wine category as opposed to a secondary offshoot. Visitors to the region will even see large billboards along the local roads proclaiming it the "land of rosé."

Geographically, Provence is a broad term that refers loosely to an area in the southeastern corner of France extending from Nice, on the Côte d'Azur, to west of the Rhône River and into the Languedoc region.

It's a land where grapevines and lavender fields dot the countryside, and thyme and rosemary grow wild on the steep hillsides. Vintners tend their gnarly vines under steely blue skies in a manner that hasn't changed much since Pope Clement V built his summer palace in Avignon back in 1309.

There are numerous Provençal *appellations,* or officially designated wine-growing areas. Côtes de Provence is among the largest, and Tavel one of the smallest. In addition to well-known Bandol, on the Mediterranean coast between Marseilles and Toulon, other appellations include Coteaux Varois, Coteaux d'Aix-en-Provence, Baux de Provence, and Cassis. Farther north are Côtes-du-Rhône Villages, Costières de Nîmes, Lirac, Côtes du Ventoux, Côtes du Lubéron, and Tavel.

Each region declares its style of rosé to be unique, based on distinct microclimates and winemaking traditions. This is known as *terroir,* a factor that gives personality and style to a wine. To make their rosés, most Provençal winemakers use various blends of grapes that include Grenache, Cinsaut, Mourvèdre, Tibouren, and sometimes Syrah and Cabernet Sauvignon.

In general, Provençal wines are quite light in color and texture. They are fresh, bright, and firm on the palate—and wonderfully suited to a variety of cuisines (see chapter 6, pages 67–68). The exception to the rule is Tavel, where the wines are generally darker and more full-bodied.

Most refreshing, in my opinion, is the widespread regional celebration of rosé. This passion for pink is particularly vivid at the Provence Center for Rosé Research in the town of Vidauban, not far from Aix-en-Provence. With its staff of fifteen, the center is the only scientific research facility in the world dedicated only to rosé. The enologists who work there spend their time investigating questions concerning wine quality as well as the culture of rosé. In their small, on-site winery, they produce some two hundred sample rosés each year for study.

Ironically, no one I've met who lives in the south of France has a really clear idea about why rosé is so important there.

"There seems to be a confluence of circumstances here," Provence Center for Rosé Research director Gilles Masson surmises. "It's got to relate to our warm weather as well as various human and economic factors." The scientist, who also owns sixty acres of grapes destined for commercial rosé, believes that the summer tourist trade long ago provoked the need for a lighter style of wine. Since most of the grapes grown in the region are red, rosé was the natural choice.

He could be right, although similar regional climates in Spain and Italy have never provoked the same massive interest in pink wine as that which is found in southern France.

Olivier Ott, whose family founded the renowned rosé winery Domaines Ott, has his own theory on the subject. "In antiquity, there was only white wine and rosé," he says. "They didn't ferment wines with their skins, which give off color. Instead they would crush the grapes and press off the juice from the skins before they took on a red hue. The wines were pink. It's no accident that the seventeenth-century Dutch painters showed mostly pink or white wines on their canvasses."

French author and director of the Interprofessional Council of Wines of Provence, François Millo, concurs, although he, too, doesn't know for sure why rosé is so popular in his home region. "It's a bit of a mystery," he notes. "Wine was first brought to Marseille around 600 B.C. by the Greeks, who founded the city. At this time and up until the Middle Ages, all wines were more or less pale in color. Between 100 B.C. and A.D. 400, wine followed the Romans in their conquest of France and arrived in the north and west. It was only well after this phase of expansion into the northern areas that red wines became widespread. However, the color pink remained in the region of French wine's origins."

Although it may be the most popular wine in Provence, rosé is rarely considered a *grand vin*— a great wine. Maybe that's because so much rosé is and has been made for simple quaffing. But as early as the nineteenth century, some rosé winemakers sought opportunities to distinguish rosé beyond its prevailing modest image. One was Alsatian-born vintner Marcel Ott, who founded Domaines Ott in 1896. The Ott winery shifted its production to focus almost exclusively on rosé in 1920. Then, in 1929, Ott's son, René, came up with a distinctive amphora-shaped bottle design that heralded the winery's rise to status as one of the region's premier rosé producers. In 2004, French Champagne house Louis Roederer acquired a proprietary interest in Domaines Ott, which typically sells for far more than most other rosés. Is it worth it? That's for you to judge. With its elegant packaging, Domaines Ott is easy to find on wineshop shelves.

Some of Domaines Ott's vineyards are located close to the quaint seaside village of Bandol, where vintner Paul Bunan also makes distinctive rosé at Domaines Bunan. Considering how long wine has been made in Provence, Bunan is a recent arrival. His winemaking family emigrated from Algeria in 1963, where they had settled in 1920.

As for the Provençal predilection for pink, Bunan says simply, "Here in the south, it's hot, and we need a cool wine to refresh ourselves. It makes sense that rosé is part of our tradition."

"But," he adds, "the notion of high quality has only come somewhat recently, with the appellation system that has put limits on our production of grapes."

Bunan is referring to the notion that overcropped vines—or those with too many grapes—produce wines lacking in flavor. A winery located in a desirable region such as Bandol cannot put the name Bandol on its label unless it conforms to the local production parameters that are designated by the state. In this way, the system attempts to guarantee a certain standard of quality typical to the region.

It's a good thing, too, because even the French have a conflicted relationship with pink wine. "There's still a negative feeling about rosé," says Daniel Ravier, the director of Domaine Tempier, also in Bandol. "The average Frenchman doesn't understand it. Consumers often think rosé is a blend of white and red wine."

Domaine Tempier, which has produced wine since 1834, is doing its best to craft rosés of distinction. Its wines are distributed widely in the United States as well as in France. In an odd twist, however, 70 percent of Tempier's wines are red, despite the fact that 70 percent of the wine made in Bandol is rosé.

But France is full of paradoxes. The country's renowned appellation system, designed to preserve benchmark quality, can also hamstring vintners who want to improve their wines through innovative winemaking techniques. Appellation laws and time-honored traditions may forbid or discourage certain methods of viticulture and vinification that New World winemakers take for granted.

In many appellations, irrigation is forbidden, ostensibly to discourage overcropping. (More water can lead to more grapes.) Unfortunately, in very hot, dry years, both vines and grapes can be damaged by lack of sufficient water. Without the ability to irrigate, many growers and their vines have suffered in a number of recent vintages.

So tradition can be a double-edged sword. With it, the French have inflicted other wounds upon themselves. One such sore spot revolves around barrel fermentation, a technique that can add richness and roundness to a wine's texture. Typically, Provençal rosés are fermented in large cement, wood, or stainless-steel tanks. Barrel fermentation of rosé is almost unheard of.

However, throughout the New World, barrel fermentation is producing wines of exceptional quality. As such, it's a technique that merits consideration. So far, the French have turned a blind eye to it. Even at the Rosé Research Center in Vidauban, virtually no research had been done on this winemaking practice when I visited in November of 2003.

Nonetheless, a number of renegade rosé producers in Provence are attempting to put a new twist on rosé methodology. It's no surprise that the innovators are often relative newcomers to the game.

Swiss-born, Canadian-educated, and New York–hardened businessman Philippe Bieler raised a few eyebrows when he purchased Château Routas, about thirty miles from Aix-en-Provence, back in 1991. He surprised his neighbors even more when he hired California winemaker Bob Lindquist, of Qupé winery, as a consultant. Lindquist brought barrel fermentation to Routas, which makes about 30 percent of its rosé blend using the technique.

In the Coteaux d'Aix, also close to Aix-en-Provence, Philippe Kessler is also pushing the envelope at Château Calissane, where he makes four different rosés. The French business-man, who has lived and worked in the United States, purchased the twenty-five-hundred-acre property in 2001. He's a relative novice to winemaking, which is probably why he's unusually open to new ideas. Although red, white, and rosé wines are made at Calissane, the round-textured rosés may be the ones that will most change the flavors of the local landscape.

But let's not denigrate tradition, per se. Without it, there would hardly be a culture of rosé in the south of France—or anywhere else in the country for that matter. If we were to mark our map with an X on the heart of a singular rosé tradition in France, it would lie on the spot marked Tavel.

It's no wonder this tiny town, with a population of only fifteen hundred, has a big name in rosé. Since rosé is the only wine that can be made from grapes grown in the appellation, Tavel's thirty-odd wineries can't afford to make anything less than exceptional pink wine.

"For us, Tavel is more than simply rosé," says Brother Roger, who has made wine at Château de Manissy since 1950. "Our style is ancestral." The wizened winemaker is also a monk. His order, Les Pères de la Sainte-Famille, has owned Château de Manissy since 1919. Brother Roger runs the winery, and his colleague, Brother Jean, works in the vineyard. With its cracked stucco walls and slightly crumbling infrastructure, Château de Manissy is a place where time seems to stand still. The wines are made in the full-bodied, darker style typical of the region.

At the other end of town, Franck Popek, of Domaine Méjan-Taulier, makes an elegant, light-textured yet fruit-driven rosé called Canto Perdrix. He's a former nuclear engineer whose wife's family has owned the vineyard and winery for generations. Popek learned his craft from his father-in-law, André Méjan.

Popek offered an interesting anecdote to explain Tavel's focus on rosé. In medieval times, the French king Philippe le Bel had a château in Tavel. But he didn't get along with the Pope, whose residence at the time was in nearby Avignon. Apparently the Pope liked his wine with a darker hue. Just to be contrary, Philippe insisted on pink, and a tradition was born.

The story seems a bit far-fetched, but Popek demonstrated Tavel's staying power in a more concrete manner when he opened a dusty, old bottle of 1954 Canto Perdrix (see page 22). Drinking that brilliant, old wine whet my appetite and led me to the Auberge de Tavel, a small restaurant in town. One-third of the wine selections there were Tavel rosés, and I picked one at random: La Dame Rousse, from Domaine de la Mordorée. Like so many well-crafted, dry pink wines, this one paired quite nicely with a plate of poached oysters wrapped in spinach, and later on, with gamey wild hare. Here in the heart of wine country, the French don't eat; they dine. And in Provence, *l'art de la table* begins with *vin rosé*.

beyond france:
OTHER EUROPEAN ROSÉS

3

It's odd to think that no European country aside from France has developed a true, broad-based culture of rosé. But that doesn't mean there are no other people in those lands who appreciate a cool, refreshing quaff of crisp, dry pink-hued wine. Spanish and Italian rosés are easy to find, even in the United States. Greek rosé is also starting to find its niche. The Portuguese, who have made their New World mark with fizzy, sweet rosés over the years, also make a little dry rosé, although it is difficult to find outside Portugal.

Here's the skinny on those European countries—France excepted—whose pink wines you are most likely to find on wineshop shelves or on your dinner table.

italy

Throughout Italy, from Piedmont in the north to Sicily in the south, each wine region offers distinct styles of wines made with traditional grape varieties. But unlike France, with its Côtes de Provence appellation dedicated almost exclusively to pink wine, Italy has no corresponding banner region for rosé, or *rosato,* as the Italians say.

Nonetheless, fine rosés are made by many Italian winemakers. Indeed, anyone in Italy who makes red wine probably makes a little *rosato,* and many of these pink wines find their way to American shores. They may range in style from the fairly full-blown Il Mimo, made in Piedmont from Nebbiolo grapes, to the lighter-styled Alois Lageder and Cantina Bolzano wines, both made in Alto Adige from Lagrein grapes. In Val d'Aosta, on the Swiss border, a barely pink wine is made from Pinot Noir, better known as the premier red grape of France's Burgundy. The Val d'Aosta version is so light in color, it could easily be confused with a white wine. Sparkling rosé is also made in Italy (see page 63).

Like the French, the Italians have a kind of de facto tradition of rosé. Prior to modern times, red grapes were pressed relatively quickly, and they typically yielded wines that were more pink than red.

In his eighteenth-century travels to northern Italy, wine lover and future United States president Thomas Jefferson described the Nebbiolo-based wines made there as sparkling and sweet. (Today's Nebbiolo is dark red and dry.) These fresh, young, pink wines were drunk soon after they were made. Some vintages were surely redder and drier than others, but there was really no distinction made between darker hues and lighter hues. It was a common theme throughout the land.

Nonetheless, some Italian winemakers have made a long-standing effort in modern times to create distinctive rosés. Perhaps the most unusual of these wines comes from Eduardo Valentini, who makes a richly textured, intensely flavored rosé from the Montepulciano grape. Valentini Cerasuolo Montepulciano d'Abruzzo may not be for everyone, however, with its high-toned aromas and even higher price tag, which rivals many of the world's more expensive red wines.

Valentini may be different, but he is no anomaly. There is a tradition of making rosé in his area, at the center of Italy. The crushed grapes are soaked in open wood casks, then pressed off the skins, and fermented in large, oval wooden tanks, which gives them a roundness and fullness on the palate.

In Bolgheri, on the Tuscan coast, the well-known Antinori wine family also makes a rosé of distinction. Oddly enough, it was the result of an accident some years back.

"The Antinoris have made wine in Bolgheri for thirty years," says Renzo Cotarella, chief winemaker and managing director for the Antinori wine business. "You could always see the signs for Rosato Antinori along the roads there."

The family's original pink wine was typically light and simple. Then, about ten years ago, the Antinoris decided to make a more "serious" red wine in the region from mostly French grapes such as Cabernet Sauvignon and Merlot. "We planted these red grapes in the wrong soils," Renzo admits, with the focus of hindsight. The grapes didn't ripen as well as hoped, so the winemaker bled off some of the pink juice from the freshly crushed grapes in order to concentrate color and flavor in the remaining juice destined for red wine (see page 13).

The pink juice was fermented as rosé, and the results were so good that the wine was given a proprietary name, Scalabrone, after a famous bandit who lived in the region in the early 1800s. Scalabrone has since become a benchmark rosé for the Antinori line.

Most Italian rosé—regardless of its region of origin—is fresh and light-textured, showing modest fruit flavors and subtle elegance. It tends to be a bit fuller on the palate than the rosé of France's premier growing region, Provence, but lighter in style than many New World rosés, such as those made in California and Australia.

spain

The Romans brought winemaking to northern Spain around 300 B.C. Needless to say, it was thoroughly embraced by the locals. If we choose to believe various wine historians who state that early winemaking techniques caused most wine to be pink, then we might surmise that rosé is the original wine of Spain. The Spanish call their rosé *rosado*. It is also occasionally referred to as *clarete*.

Unfortunately, Spanish wine lovers took a hit for some five hundred years beginning in the eighth century, when the Moors dominated Spain and discouraged wine consumption. Apparently the French clergy saw an opportunity to harass their Muslim neighbors by surreptitiously entering the country to plant grapevines. By the time the Christians regained their political dominance in 1492, Spanish winegrowers were poised to assume their previous preeminent position in a land where the culture of wine could be fully celebrated.

Still, except for in the south of Spain, where an ongoing brisk international trade with the British occurred, winemaking throughout the country remained somewhat backward until recently. Today's relative internal political calm and fiscal prosperity have led Spanish winemakers to explore their traditional grapes and winemaking customs alongside newer methods and varietals hailing from France and other parts of the world.

Unlike France, however, Spain has no wine-growing region dedicated to rosé. In Rioja, one of the largest wine regions in the country, rosé is nonetheless very much a local drink appreciated with gusto during the hot summer months. Local winemakers will often blend a white grape called Viura with red grapes such as Tempranillo and Garnacha to lighten their wines for this seasonal approach. Best known among the Rioja rosés is Muga, which is made in this manner.

Just north of Rioja, Navarra is Spain's best known region for pink wines, made mostly with red Garnacha (or Grenache) grapes. Look for wines from Ochoa, a winery that makes one of the region's better pink wines. Vega Sindoa, also in Navarra, makes a very good rosé from both Garnacha and Cabernet Sauvignon grapes as well.

The Catalunya district—also linked to the Priorat area—is another locale that produces fine rosé. Oddly enough, one of the most widely known carries a French name, René Barbier. In the 1980s, Barbier came to Priorat from France with a number of friends to jump-start the then sleepy wine area. His efforts have paid off, particularly with his refreshing rosé made from a blend of Garnacha, Tempranillo, and Cariñena grapes.

It's hard to ascribe any particular unifying style to Spanish *rosado*. Like good rosés every-where, they tend to be light-textured, with good acidity and subtle cherry and raspberry flavors. In comparison to French rosés, the Spanish wines often display rounder texture with more fruit-forward flavors.

greece

Like the Romans, the Greeks benefit from one of the oldest wine cultures in the world. It's no wonder that Greece boasts more than three hundred ancient indigenous grape varieties, many of which are used to make rosé.

Indeed, the nation's long-standing love affair with wine has created a widespread culture of home winemaking, in which dry rosé plays an important role. From a consumer's perspective, visitors to any small-town Greek taverna are likely to find only two wines served: rosé or the ubiquitous semisweet and resinous retsina.

And yet Greek wines remain far from ubiquitous in America. "Greek wines have a bad reputation because of retsina," says Elias Karkabasis, a six-foot, nine-inch former basketball player who now imports wine in the United States and Canada. "It's our national Greek tragedy," he says with a lighthearted laugh.

Actually, retsina can be a delightfully refreshing wine, particularly as an aperitif before a meal. But its distinctive and forward flavors don't always play well to American tastes.

As a result, a new wave in Greek wine is now making its way to the United States, and a small percentage are rosés. They tend to be made by Greek winemakers who have studied or worked abroad in places like France or California. The well-traveled wine professionals have come home to put an international stamp on the wines that have been drunk there traditionally.

Among them is a wine from Gaia Estate on the Peloponnese Peninsula that boasts the largest number of Greek wine appellations. The wine is called Agiorgitiko 14-18h, hardly a name that flows easily off our Anglophonic tongues. But the wine coats the palate without a hitch, showing bright-textured mineral and herb flavors backed by cherry and citrus overtones. The moniker refers to the grape variety, Agiorgitiko, and a winemaking technique that allows the grape skins to macerate for fourteen to eighteen hours prior to fermentation.

Another wine to look for is Meliasto, from Domaine Spiropoulos, also in the Peloponnese. The winery has been growing grapes organically for more than a decade and produces a very light-textured wine that serves up a solid core of strawberry, grapefruit, and mineral flavors. It is made from the Moscofilero grape, a very light colored grape that is also used to make white wines.

Xynomavro is yet another Greek grape fairly unknown to Americans. With its pronounced acidity and robust tannins, Xynomavro is often compared to Nebbiolo, the premier red grape of Italy's Barolo region. Xynomavro also makes a fine rosé, produced by Kir-Yianni and bottled under the Akakies label.

These wines are much easier to drink than they are to pronounce. They are priced quite reasonably and are worth exploring should you discover them at your local wineshop.

germany

With a fine wine tradition steeped in Riesling and—to a lesser degree—other white varietals such as Gewürztraminer, Müller-Thurgau, and Scheurebe, Germany produces some of the most extraordinary white wines in the world. Due to the relatively cold climate, growing later-ripening red grapes is quite a challenge for German vintners.

Nonetheless, they try (with varying degrees of success) with small quantities of red varieties such as Pinot Noir (called *Spätburgunder*), Portugieser, Lemburger, Trollinger, and Pinot Meunier (called *Schwarzriesling*). All of these red grapes are suitable for making rosé, traditionally known as *Weissherbst* and typically made from only one grape variety at a time. (Neighboring Austria also makes a small amount of rosé, called *Schilcher*.)

Weissherbst is almost always made in a fairly sweet style and balanced by brisk acidity. However, some vintners as of late have begun making *Weissherbst* in a dry style. Rainer Lingenfelder is one of them. He makes his dry rosé from Pinot Noir. "In Germany, sometimes rosé is the result of a questionable harvest," Lingentelder says. "But after I visited Montpellier, in southern France, I decided to make some rosé myself. My first vintage was in 1994."

Lingenfelder crushes his red grapes and lets the skins macerate overnight before bleeding a small portion of the juice to be fermented as pink wine. The public's response was quite favorable, and the wine—made in an elegant style—is now sold throughout Germany. But don't look too hard for Lingenfelder rosé or any other German *Weissherbst* in America. Precious few find their way to the New World.

portugal

It's ironic to think that the country that has shaped American perception of rosé over the last fifty years drinks very little pink wine at home. Portugal, best known for its richly textured sweet, red Ports, also makes many lovely dry wines—both red and white. Vinho Verde, a simple wine made to be drunk when it is young, fills the local niche that might otherwise be occupied by dry rosé. Still, a few dry pink wines are produced in Portugal, but they are rarely found on the U.S. market. Typically, those dry Portuguese rosés that find their way into the United States are very inexpensive and straightforward in style.

But two brands made in a sweet style, mainly for export—Lancers and Mateus—have claimed an important market share in America for more than a half century. And although these wines are not made in a manner that reflects the quality aspired to by most of the wines featured in this book, they merit discussion by virtue of their broad distribution. Both are sweet and marked by a slight effervescence. Aside from the bubbles, they are somewhat akin to California-grown White Zinfandel (see page 48). Lancers is made from grape concentrate in a year-round production effort that pays little heed to the concept of vintage. Mateus follows a similar philosophy.

According to Lancers director of sales and marketing, Antonio Lopes Vieria, Lancers was developed to appeal to American military servicemen toward the end of World War II. "It was thought that the soldiers who had discovered wine in Europe would still want something easy to drink that was semisweet and with bubbles—like Coca-Cola," Lopes Vieria explains. The name Lancers was inspired from a Velásquez painting entitled "Las Lanzas." Lancers was launched in America in 1944 by founders Henry Behar, an American, and Portuguese winemaker Antonio Soares Franco. That year, they sold 400 cases of wine in the United States. By 1964, Lancers was selling 400,000 cases annually and had become the nation's number one wine import.

Mateus predates Lancers by two years. It was founded in 1942 by Fernando van Zeller Guedes as the anchor product for a wide range of wines marketed under the Sogrape umbrella company.

White Zinfandel ultimately usurped a significant number of Mateus and Lancers fans. Today, for example, Lancers sales in the U.S. have dwindled to 100,000 cases, still an impressive number. Oddly enough, the brand's biggest market is now in Italy. A small amount is sold in Portugal, mostly to foreign tourists.

4 new world rosés

New World winemakers are always ready for a challenge. They have clearly decided that the French and their European neighbors needn't have a monopoly on dry pink wine. Accordingly, the New World's appreciation of fine rosé continues to grow.

As a result, a fairly riotous parade of New World rosé labels has appeared on the scene. California leads the charge, with a bevy of new wines cropping up each year. California vintners have been followed by Northwest winemakers from Washington and Oregon. On the East Coast, a few New Yorkers and Virginians are dabbling in rosé as well, although not enough is made to leave local markets. Even Texas winemakers have now started to think pink.

And why shouldn't they? Rosé and barbecue is a match made in heaven. The Texans' neighbors in Mexico's Baja Peninsula have also followed suit, while Australians and a few South Americans now send a selection of pink wines north after each Down Under harvest. They keep the market supplied with fresh, new wines for us to taste year-round.

Nonetheless, dry rosé's popularity among New World winemakers is a new development. It's probably due to the fact that few wine lovers in the United States or Australia traditionally drink it. There seems to be a stigma associated with the sweet, pink, and slightly effervescent wines produced by Portuguese wineries such as Lancers and Mateus, which for many years have been widely distributed throughout the United States. Because of their pink color, these wines have created confusion among many wine drinkers who have assumed all pink wines are made in the same style. White Zinfandel—technically a rosé, too—hasn't helped raise consumer consciousness to the dry paradigm either. In fact, White Zinfandel has reinforced the impression left by Lancers and Mateus.

The good news is that with more serious New World winemakers entering the rosé market, we are witnessing an ever-increasing availability of high quality rosés. To my palate, the thought is a refreshing one.

california

Of all the New World wine regions, California has had the biggest impact on the culture of pink wine.

Rosé isn't new to the West Coast. Two large, well-known wineries—Simi and Joseph Phelps—were among those ahead of the curve more than a decade ago. Simi, in Sonoma County, first made a fresh, light-textured rosé from Cabernet Sauvignon beginning in 1988. But the winery discontinued it in 1997 due to a lack of consumer interest.

For much of the 1990s, Joseph Phelps Winery, in Napa Valley, also made a zippy, fruity rosé from Grenache grapes grown in the Monterey area. It, too, met the same fate as Simi's Cabernet rosé. The U.S. palate—or psyche—wasn't buying it.

Ironically, California's "accidental" pink wine—White Zinfandel—was growing exponentially at this time to become one of the nation's top selling wines. The story is fairly well known. In the early 1970s, Sutter Home Winery, in Napa Valley, specialized in red wines made from Zinfandel. The winery also made a small amount of dry rosé using Zinfandel as well.

But in 1975, the rosé fermentation stuck; that is to say, the fermentation yeast were unable to convert all of the natural sugars in the juice to alcohol, and the wine remained somewhat sweet.

On the advice of their friend and well-known Sacramento wine retailer Darrell Corti, Sutter Home's owners—the Trinchero family—bottled their sweet Zinfandel rosé anyway. To their surprise, it was received enthusiastically. (Perhaps the Trincheros shouldn't have been so surprised. The Portuguese were already doing big business at the time with Lancers and Mateus [see page 43], two sweet, pink wines made primarily for the U.S. market.)

Within fifteen years, annual production of Sutter Home White Zinfandel grew from a few thousand cases to nearly four million, making the Trinchero family one of most successful families in American wine. Other wineries followed suit, and White Zinfandel has become a California standard—sweet, inexpensive, and generally well suited to an American palate more accustomed to soda pop than wine.

Although it doesn't taste like a dry rosé table wine, there is nothing inherently wrong with White Zinfandel. In addition, there is no reason that fine, dry rosé cannot be made from Zinfandel grapes. Indeed, some are.

But in a kind of self-fulfilling prophecy, White Zinfandel is priced so low that economics require it be made with inexpensive, low-quality grapes grown from high-yielding vines. These grapes tend to be bland and unripe, a characteristic that can extend to the wine.

To make up for its lack of character, White Zinfandel is fairly well-manipulated. Its sugar content and color are carefully monitored to create a consistent beverage regardless of vintage. Fermentation may or may not be stopped early, as was the case in the original White Zin. More often than not, sweetness is added back to the wine by using grape concentrate and other grape-based sweeteners. This leads to sugar levels far in excess of those that might be found in dry-styled wines.

From a visual perspective, White Zinfandel's color may also be enhanced with commercially produced, grape-based coloring agents. Ultimately, what the finished wine lacks in ripeness, finesse, and complexity is made up for by sweetness. And that sweetness has tickled the palate of millions of Americans.

Some vintners like to say that White Zinfandel has acted as a bridge to bring the American general public into the fine wine fold. To a degree, it may be true. But the downside of White Zinfandel's widespread success is that it has caused many Americans to assume that all pink wine is the same. As a result, wine drinkers have been discouraged from investigating the other side of pink.

Fortunately, growing wine sophistication throughout the New World has set the stage for the next wave of rosé winemakers. Their dry rosés are now being snapped up with increasing enthusiasm throughout the nation.

- CALIFORNIA: TRENDSETTERS AND ICONOCLASTS

Winemaker Randall Grahm has made a career of taking the road less traveled and turning it into a superhighway. Under his Bonny Doon label, he began making high-end wines from relatively unpopular grape varieties in the early 1980s. Today many of those grapes, such as the Rhône varieties Syrah and Roussanne, are prized among both winemakers and wine lovers alike.

Grahm also makes a nice rosé. In fact, he makes four of them. Three are still wines and one is slightly bubbly, made in the style of Italian *frizzante*. Best known is Bonny Doon Vin Gris de Cigare, which is made from a blend of Grenache, Syrah, Mourvèdre, and Cinsaut grapes.

Bonny Doon's *vin gris* is made from the bled juice (see page 13) of red grapes used in his winery's Bonny Doon Le Cigare Volant. "We bleed the juice every year to improve the quality of the red wine. And as a result, we make a fine rosé too," Grahm notes. He says he was inspired by the rosés of southern France and a few unusual wines that were made in California, such as a now-forgotten rosé made by neighboring Santa Cruz Mountains winemaker David Bruce in the 1970s.

Through his efforts, Grahm has helped pave the way for a New World awakening to dry rosé. He made his first in 1982 from Pinot Noir grapes. By 1984, he had moved on to Mourvèdre, which was once widely planted in California and called Mataro. Despite the popularity of sweeter White Zinfandel, the early vintages of Bonny Doon's dry Vin Gris de Cigare met with great success—though hardly on the scale of Sutter Home.

In Grahm's pink-hued wake, other winemakers tentatively followed. Saintsbury, in northern California's Carneros district, made its first rosé from Pinot Noir grapes in 1989. In this case, it was not the French, but an Australian, who spurred the project on. "Our rosé was inspired by a conversation I had with (Australian winemaker and wine writer) James Halliday," Saintsbury co-owner David Graves recalls. "We were at a Pinot Noir conference in Oregon when he brought up the subject. Then, in 1989, we had a large crop that was rained on." To intensify the red wine, Graves bled off a small amount of pink juice to ferment separately and called the result Vincent Vin Gris. "The name was actually our graphic designer's idea," Graves admits. Since then, Saintsbury has made the wine every year.

The list continues to expand to include winemakers from all of the state's many wine regions. Like Bonny Doon and Saintsbury, most make their blush wines as a by-product of red wine production (see page 14). It's a time-honored method that produces small quantities of high quality wine.

Because of their state's sunny disposition, California winemakers often make their dry rosés from grapes that are riper than those made by their European colleagues. These New World wines are fuller bodied and somewhat more fruit-driven. The biggest problem with these artisanal small-batch rosés is that there is not much to go around. Many winemakers produce only a few hundred cases. But some have discovered—much to their amazement—that they are selling out of rosé faster than they anticipated. Plans for increased production are in the works.

That's the case with Napa Valley vintner Rob Sinskey, who began making a tiny amount of rosé from Pinot Noir back in 1989. Unlike many winemakers, Sinskey doesn't bleed his juice, but simply makes his rosé as he would a white wine, such as Chardonnay. Instead of crushing his grapes and allowing a short maceration of the skins in the juice, he gently presses the whole grape clusters to produce a wine that is quite light in color, almost strawlike, but with a faint salmon hue.

SOLOROSA

SoloRosa is a California rosé that I make in partnership with my friend and colleague Daniel Moore. Without SoloRosa, the inspiration, energy, and focus required to write this book could never have been harnessed.

In Italian, *solo rosa* means "only pink." The name came to me in a dream, despite the fact that I don't even speak Italian. In 2000, I made a prototype barrel of rosé, but I couldn't figure out what to call it. Then, in one of those "Eureka!" moments, I woke up one night with the words *"solo rosa"* running through my head. It was only later on that an Italian friend told me exactly what the words meant. The name stuck, albeit with my own quirky styling.

The roots of SoloRosa actually stretch back to 1973, when I moved to Nice, France, to study music at the National Conservatory there. Judging from my first two-franc meal at the student cafeteria, it was clear I had been eating poorly most of my American life. Not surprisingly, my appetite for the cuisine and the wines of southern France evolved faster than my musical skills.

Returning to the United States some five years later, I spent most of my free time seeking out flavors that reminded me of the dishes I had enjoyed on France's Côte d'Azur. Many of those meals in France were accompanied by local rosés.

I worked for another decade as a musician, splitting my time between New York and France. But a 1987 gig as bandleader at the Grand Casino in Monte Carlo confirmed what I had suspected all along: eating and drinking interested me more than music—at least professionally. So I changed gears and took a job as cellar rat at a small winery on Long Island, New York, to learn a new craft from the ground up.

In New York, we bled our unfermented Merlot juice from the rainy 1989 vintage to increase its intensity (see page 13). Then we pumped the pink bleed into a few old barrels and left them in a forgotten corner of the winery. The juice fermented into an elegant rosé that reminded me of some of my favorite French wines. It had a touch more body, however, and a smooth, creamy texture that I now know came from the barrel fermentation. We never actually sold that wine, but instead, drank it up ourselves!

A few years later, I shifted direction again and became a wine writer. *Wine Spectator* magazine hired me to cover the West Coast wine scene and sent me from New York out to San Francisco in 1995. Five years later, I made another leap of faith and moved to the Napa Valley to work for gourmet food and wine purveyor Dean & DeLuca, which had opened up a West Coast branch in the heart of the wine country.

Napa Valley's siren call to make wine was irresistible, and I made an initial barrel of SoloRosa from local Sangiovese grapes, using techniques similar to those learned during my Long Island days. My friend Daniel Moore helped me finish and bottle the wine. Like that early Long Island rosé, it was never sold. But the 2000 SoloRosa was so popular among our friends, we decided to make a commercial release the following year. Daniel's Gewürztraminers (under his Z-Moore label) had always been exceptional, as were his Russian River Valley Chardonnays and Pinot Noirs. It was exciting for both of us to stretch out into the realm of serious pink wine.

As partners in pink, we made fifty barrels of 2001 SoloRosa using a blend of mostly Sangiovese, Syrah, and Merlot. The incredibly positive response among consumers and the national media exceeded our expectations. Today we're slowly increasing production to satisfy demand.

Looking back, it seems as though many of my winemaker friends and colleagues must have had a simultaneously similar notion. The market is now blessed with an increasingly diverse array of rosés hailing from all over the New World.

"We've always done it this way, and it seems to work well," Sinskey explains. It's not uncommon to find European winemakers who make rosé in a similar manner, which yields equally pale-hued wines.

"My wife, Maria, is a chef," Sinskey says. "She finds that rosé is an incredibly flexible wine. It goes with so many of the grilled foods and fresh ingredients that are a part of our evolving California cooking tradition."

australia

On the other side of the globe, Australian wine writer Max Allen has also noticed a distinct rise in interest for dry rosé in the last several years. Typically, Australian rosé has issued from the warmer Barossa and McLaren Vale regions. But, as in California, renewed consumer consumption has inspired vintners all over the continent to experiment.

At Allen's Divine Pink Wine Party, a triennial blind taste-off that pits most of the rosés available in the country against each other, the writer reports that overall wine quality has consistently improved for Australia's domestic producers. True to form, the Aussies have incorporated their classic sense of humor into their wine labels, with such titles as "Bloodwood Big Men in Tights" and "Wirra Wirra Mrs. Wigley," the latter named for the winery cat. Unfortunately, few of the Australian pinks are currently available outside of Australia.

As with all fine rosés, the best offer a certain complexity of style that may include mineral, citrus, and earth components as well as primary cherry and raspberry notes. Stylistically, most of the better New World rosés are dry, or nearly so, although some retain a touch of residual sugar to enhance the fruit. They still taste refreshingly on the dry side, nonetheless. Truly sweet rosés like White Zinfandel—which may contain as much as 3.5 percent residual sugar—really belong in a separate category.

5 sparkling rosés

Much of the world's sparkling rosé comes from the Champagne region in France, which is possibly the only area outside of southern France truly renowned for its pink wine tradition. However, Italy and Spain both produce noteworthy pink bubblies, as do certain New World regions, especially California.

As with still rosé wines, sparkling rosé can take its pale hue from the *saignée* method (see page 13), which involves limited skin contact with red grapes, such as Pinot Noir or Pinot Meunier. However, many top producers in Champagne prefer to forego the *saignée* technique in favor of blending a small portion of non-sparkling red wine into their otherwise white wine base, which may also contain a significant amount of Chardonnay. In addition to adding a pink hue to the wine, it is believed that this method gives greater complexity to the blend.

france

Sparkling wine is made throughout France, but nearly all of the sparkling rosé you'll find in America comes from Champagne, the French capital of bubbly. Only about 3 percent of the Champagne exported to the United States is actually pink. Nonetheless, pink wine has long been a part of Champagne's regional heritage. One of the earliest known recorded sales transactions for Champagne rosé is linked to a sales slip from Veuve Cliquot Ponsardin dated 1775, which listed a delivery of seventy-five bottles to a Monsieur Godinot in Reims. As early as 1814, the celebrated Parisian restaurant Les Frères Provençaux offered *vin rosé mousseux* (sparkling rosé) on its wine list.

But because so little pink Champagne is produced relative to white Champagne, the locals charge a premium for it. Fortunately, Champagne rosé is not always très expensive, as it is made in all three quality tiers: non-vintage, vintage-dated, and prestige cuvée. The most modest prices will generally come from the non-vintage wines, or those wines made from a blend of several different vintages. At the opposite end of the price spectrum lie the prestige cuvée wines, such as Krug and Dom Perignon. These often can be found for vertiginously high sums well over a hundred dollars per bottle, making them the most expensive category of rosé in the world.

The Champagne region lies in northern France, about an hour's train ride east of Paris. Residents of Champagne will remind you with great regularity that only those sparkling wines made in their own wine region can be legitimately called "Champagne." It's true. But many fine sparkling wines are made outside of Champagne as well. Most of the best ones—both in and outside of Champagne—are made by using what is known as the *méthode champenoise*—or Champagne method—which was devised in Champagne in the early eighteenth century.

- THE CHAMPAGNE METHOD

The Champagne method involves two distinct fermentations: one in a traditional tank or barrel, and a second one in the same bottle that you ultimately open at home with a pop. The second fermentation produces those classic bubbles.

All wine fermentations yield carbon dioxide, which bubbles to the surface of an open tank, barrel, or wineglass and exits into the air. Once the fermentation—the result of yeast consuming natural sugars in grape juice—is complete, no more carbon dioxide is produced. Eventually it escapes into the surrounding atmosphere, and the wine becomes a still, or flat, wine.

That's also what happens at first with Champagne and other similarly made sparkling wines. The initial dry, still wine is produced and then set into thick, pressure resistant bottles. A little more sugar and yeast are subsequently introduced into the bottle, which is tightly sealed with either a cork or bottle cap. As the new yeast chows down on the sugar, it creates new carbon dioxide bubbles, which can't escape from the sealed bottle and thus remain in solution. The yeasts eventually die and slowly slide into the neck of the bottle, where they create a sediment plug.

When the winemaker determines it is time to finish the wine, the bottle cap is removed. Pressure from the carbon dioxide gas in solution causes the yeast plug to be expelled. Then the bottle is resealed with a traditional cork. Just prior to resealing the bottle, the winemaker may add a small *dosage,* or some sweetened wine, to round out the wine's pronounced acidity. In most cases, the sparkling wine still remains fairly dry, a quality often signified by the word "brut" on the label.

Because the Champagne method is a time-consuming, labor-intensive process, not all sparkling wine is made in this manner. A technique called the "bulk process" is more commonly used for less-expensive wines. Here, the secondary fermentation occurs in a pressurized tank—not in individual bottles. Wines made in this manner do not typically have the same complexity of flavor as those wines made in the Champagne method. But they can, nonetheless, be quite good.

While most still rosés are released within six months to a year of production, sparkling rosés made in the Champagne method require a longer time in the bottle before finding their way to the marketplace. It costs a winemaker money to store inventory, which is one more reason that sparkling rosé generally costs more than still rosé.

california

Unlike the French, Americans have only recently begun to embrace sparkling rosé as a serious wine category. With some notable exceptions, it's no accident that many of California's sparkling wineries were founded by French Champagne houses. Traditionally, Americans did not have an equally keen interest in bubbly.

One of these French-owned wineries, Roederer Estate, is located in northern California's Anderson Valley. The winery's French-born winemaker, Arnaud Weyrich, was at first mystified by American visitors' initial reactions to his well-crafted pink California sparkling wine. "When I first came here, about ten years ago," he recalls, "most customers wouldn't even try our sparkling rosé. Now, more and more people are accepting it." As a result, the winery has increased its production.

Nearly all of California's sparkling wine houses now make pink bubbly. Most are made with the traditional Champagne grapes—Pinot Noir, Pinot Meunier, and Chardonnay. Typically, these grapes are grown in the cooler regions of the state, such as Carneros and the Sonoma and Central Coasts. As a result, this is where many of the wineries are located. They include such producers as Domaine Carneros, Gloria Ferrer, Korbel, Pacific Echo, and Laetitia.

However, upper Napa Valley boasts three seminal sparkling wineries: Schramsberg and S. Anderson (founded by Americans) and Domaine Chandon (which is French-owned). The three wineries were among the first in modern-day California to make sparkling wine using the Champagne method. All three make sparkling rosé as well. See page 114 for a more complete listing of those wineries that make sparkling rosé.

italy and spain

Italy and Spain don't have the rosé tradition that France does, but the two countries still produce some lovely sparkling pink wines.

Italy has a number of words to designate sparkling wine. Most common are *spumante* and *frizzante*. *Spumante* is more typically made in the style associated with Champagne. Some of the better producers come from the northern region of Trentino-Alto Adige.

Italy's *frizzantes* are in a class all their own. This style of sparkling wine is really a semi-sparkling wine—that is, less bubbly than those wines made with the Champagne or bulk methods. Because they are bottled under less pressure, *frizzante* wines do not require the sturdy bottles and corks typical of Champagne. In fact, they often have the same bottle design as still wines, so you may have to look carefully for them on wineshop shelves. *Frizzante* is typically a light-textured wine that makes a terrific aperitif. The wines are generally somewhat sweet and low in alcohol.

The Spanish make sparkling wines using the Champagne method and call them *cava*. The term, which means "cellar," was adopted some thirty-five years ago to avoid confusing Spanish sparkling wines with French Champagne. Many are quite good, and often come at a price tag that beats their French counterparts. Ironically, the world's two largest sparkling wine producers—Freixenet and Codorniu—are Spanish and not French. But less than 1 percent of all *cava* is pink.

Most *cava* is made in the Penedès region of Catalonia, although it is also produced in the regions of Valencia, Aragon, Navarra, and Rioja.

See page 116 for tasting notes on Italian and Spanish sparkling wines.

6 recipes for rosé

Americans have only recently begun to appreciate rosé's wide-ranging food affinities. Perhaps New World wine lovers have been put off by the erroneous perception that all pink wines are sweet and therefore not suitable for a "serious" meal. To its credit, a Napa Valley restaurant called Cindy's Backstreet Kitchen has created a monthlong, summertime rosé promotion called "Don't Be Afraid of Pink Wine," which features ten different rosés by the glass. Just down the street from Cindy's, the Wine Spectator Restaurant at Greystone—at the Culinary Institute of America's West Coast campus— offers twelve different California dry rosés year-round, illuminating the fact that rosé is not just for summer drinking. These two restaurants present consumers with a fabulous opportunity to sample numerous styles of what may be the world's most misunderstood or overlooked dining beverage.

Depending on where and how it is made, dry rosé can be bright, fresh, and mineral-like on the palate, or full-bodied, rich, and fruity. And while certain wine regions may be marked by a regional style, there are many exceptions to any trend. That's why it helps to taste a wine prior to pairing it with a favorite dish. When tasting prior to purchase is not an option, it's safe to assume that rosés from France, Spain, Italy, and other cooler climates tend to be brighter and more mineral-like than those wines from warmer regions such as California and Australia (warm weather produces riper grapes that yield more fruit flavors and fuller body). What's most important to remember is that rosé is a category, not a varietal, and thus comes in a very broad spectrum of styles.

pairing food and wine

Wine's natural acidity gives it an edge over other mealtime beverages. This acidity deftly complements the natural oils and fats found in most foods. As a result, a sip of fine wine leaves the palate refreshed and ready for another bite of solid sustenance.

Pairing food and wine needn't be complicated. It's not so much about flavor as it is about style. Is a wine bright and fresh tasting? Then it's probably got high acidity and low alcohol. We call that a light-bodied wine. On the other hand, a wine's texture may appear rich, round, and almost creamy on the palate. That's a full-bodied wine. The same principles of style apply to what we eat. Some dishes are heavy or rich, while others are leaner and lighter.

As a general principle, it's safe to say that similar styles of wine and food work well in tandem. A richly textured, full-bodied red wine teams up well with a robust steak or stew. A light-edged white wine pairs well with lighter seafood or vegetarian dishes. Rosé lies somewhere in the middle and may fit both ends of the style spectrum.

These are not hard-and-fast rules, of course. They are simply guidelines. There are plenty of full-bodied red wines to pair with meaty fish, such as tuna. And there are full-bodied white wines that work just fine with many meats. Ultimately, a wine's color doesn't count as much as its character.

"Why is there rosé?" asks Olivier Ott, of the eponymous French rosé family (see page 29). "Because," he explains, "there is *la soupe de poissons, les beignets de fleurs de courgettes, les farcis, la pissaladière,* and *la socca.*" Ott recites a litany of his favorite Provençal foods, which—not surprisingly—pair perfectly with the fresh, crisp, dry rosés of his native land.

It's not only Provençal cooking that teams up well with this versatile wine. Rosé's culinary affinities extend far beyond the borders of Languedoc and the Côte d'Azur. Sitting solidly in the stylistic center, many rosés can match a broad array of foods. It's safe to say that a well-made rosé will offer good, crisp acidity, which makes the category a little more akin to white wine than red wine. Rosé's firm acidity is what makes it taste good when chilled. This brightness on the palate also marries well with most seafood, just about anything made with a tomato sauce, endless vegetarian dishes, chicken, turkey, and of course cheese. But those rosés with moderate to full body and an occasional hint of tannic grip can stand up to dishes that would cause a white wine to pale. You'll probably find more of these robust rosés coming from the New World than the Old World. Ribs, lamb chops, burgers, stews, steaks, pork, duck, and goose are all easily matched with dry pink wines of this nature.

Dry rosé can also stand in quite nicely with cuisines that do not traditionally include a strong wine component. For example, Thai, Indian, and Szechwan cooking—often imbued with a spicy flair—pair with the cool, crisp flavors of a fine-tuned rosé in a masterful manner rarely matched by red wines. Lightweight white wines might not be able to stand up as well to the forceful nature of these tangy, flavorful culinary traditions either. Sometimes, only rosé will do.

And for dessert? All dry wines are challenged by sweetness, and rosé is no exception. At meal's end, you can dip your biscotti in the remainder of your rosé for a satisfying bite. But really sweet things will hardly enhance what's in your glass. That said, if you're enjoying your dessert and your rosé together, why worry? Life is too short to get hung up on convention.

recipes

Because rosé is so widely appreciated in southern France, it's natural that many dishes featured here take inspiration from Provence. Other Mediterranean countries, such as Spain and Italy, offer flavors that are equally well suited to rosé. Some Asian and Mexican spices can also pair deliriously with dry pink wine.

marinated olives with lemon and herbs

As you drive through the wine regions of Provence, Italy, or California, you'll see stands of olive trees lining the roads. At the table, rosé and olives make equally good companions. Tangy, briny-edged cured olives team up handily with a glass of cool, bright rosé as an aperitif before dinner or an afternoon snack.

To add interest to your store-bought, brined olives, toss them in a bit of olive oil, lemon zest, and herbs.

1 cup unpitted firm green or black olives such as Niçoise or Kalamata

1 tablespoon extra-virgin olive oil

1 tablespoon grated or finely chopped lemon zest

1/4 teaspoon dried thyme or 1/2 teaspoon chopped fresh rosemary

- In a small bowl, toss all the ingredients together. When serving, remember to provide a small bowl for the pits.

makes 1 cup; serves 4 as an appetizer

pissaladière (FRENCH ONION PIZZA)

This cheeseless pizza is made with the staples of a southern French kitchen: olive oil, olives, onions, garlic, and the herb that gives the hills of Provence their heady fragrance—thyme. Don't be fooled into thinking this onion pizza is sharp or bitter. The onions are caramelized and serve up a seductive blend of sweet and savory flavors that pair deliciously with dry rosé's subtle fruit and tangy mineral notes.

In France, *pissaladière* is enjoyed as a snack or before a meal. Because it is equally good when hot or at room temperature, it makes a perfect appetizer when cut into small, easy-to-hold portions. But it also can be enjoyed as a main-course pie served in wedges or squares, eaten with a knife and fork and accompanied by a green salad.

The pizza's odd-sounding name comes from *pissalat,* an anchovy purée from Nice that traditionally topped the onions. Today, anchovy fillets have replaced the purée, but those with an aversion to anchovies can dispense with them altogether.

You can shorten this recipe considerably by buying freshly made pizza dough from your local pizzeria. But the dough is not difficult to prepare; just remember you'll have to let it rise. Don't roll it out too thin, or you may find that your pizza slices will fall apart easily. To make the crust, I like to blend a little high-gluten (also called hard-wheat) flour with all-purpose flour for a chewier consistency. (Don't confuse this with gluten flour, or vital wheat gluten, which is pure gluten used as an additive or to make seitan.)

FOR THE DOUGH:

1 envelope (2 1/2 teaspoons) active dry yeast

1 1/4 cups warm water

1/2 cup high-gluten flour (see recipe introduction)

2 cups unbleached all-purpose flour, plus extra for kneading and rolling

2 tablespoons extra-virgin olive oil, plus extra for the bowl and pans

1/2 teaspoon salt

Cornmeal for the work surface (optional)

(CONTINUED)

FOR THE TOPPING:

6 tablespoons extra-virgin olive oil

8 cloves garlic, minced

2 1/2 tablespoons dried thyme

8 large onions, halved and thinly sliced

2 teaspoons salt

1 teaspoon freshly ground pepper

2 tins (6 ounces each) olive oil–packed anchovy fillets, drained (optional)

20 to 30 Niçoise olives or Kalamata olives

TO MAKE THE DOUGH:

- In a large bowl, combine the yeast with 1 cup of the warm water. Using a wooden spoon, stir in the high-gluten flour. Add the 2 cups all-purpose flour, the 2 tablespoons olive oil, and the salt. Stir with the wooden spoon until a sticky dough begins to form on the bottom of the bowl. Add the remaining 1/4 cup warm water and, using your hands, shape the dough into a large ball.

- When your hands become too sticky with dough, dust them with a little all-purpose flour. Continue kneading the dough in the bowl, pushing it down with the heel of your hand, then pulling it together in a mound and repeating until the dough becomes firm yet elastic, 4 to 5 minutes.

- Lightly oil the surface of a large bowl. Place the dough in the bowl, cover the bowl with plastic wrap, and set it in a reasonably warm room to rise for 2 hours. It should double in size. (Standard room temperature of 70°F is adequate. Cooler temperatures will delay the rising process.)

- Have ready two nonstick 12- to 14-inch round pizza pans or two 9-by-13-inch baking pans. If you do not have nonstick pans, oil each pan with 1 teaspoon olive oil. Lightly flour a work surface or, for a crust with a crunchy exterior, dust it with cornmeal. Remove the risen dough from the bowl, set it on the prepared surface, and cut it in half.

(If not using the dough immediately, place each half in a separate lightly oiled bowl. Cover the bowls with plastic wrap and place in the refrigerator for up to 8 hours. The dough will continue to rise somewhat, so use large bowls. For longer storage, wrap the dough in plastic or place it in a zippered plastic bag and freeze for up to 2 months.)

• Using a rolling pin, roll out one dough portion to fit your pans and raise the entire edge of the crust with your thumbs to make a rim. Transfer to one of the pans. Repeat with the remaining dough portion and pan.

TO MAKE THE TOPPING:

• In a large skillet or sauté pan, heat the olive oil over medium heat. Add the garlic and thyme and stir for 30 seconds. Add the onions, separating the slices with a wooden spoon and stirring so that they are evenly coated with the oil, garlic, and thyme. Add the salt and pepper and stir well. Reduce the heat to low and cook, stirring every 5 minutes until the onions are very soft and fairly translucent, about 20 minutes.

• While the onions are cooking, preheat the oven to 500°F.

• Spread the cooked onions evenly over the prepared pizza crusts. If using the anchovy fillets, arrange them on top in a diamond pattern. Dot with the olives. Bake until the rims of the crusts are golden brown, 12 to 15 minutes. Serve hot, warm, or at room temperature.

makes two 12- to 14-inch pizzas

a perfect sandwich for rosé

Rosé is a classic accompaniment for picnics and other casual lunch settings. But in my Napa Valley neighborhood, when I order a simple sandwich made only with butter and prosciutto, I'm consistently met with a surprised stare.

"That's all you want?" asks the person behind the sandwich counter.

"Yes," I reply. "With sweet butter, please."

The sweet butter always throws them, too. Usually, if they have any butter at all, it's salted. And that's not exactly what I favor with salty ham.

Americans heap mounds of diverse ingredients on their sandwiches. They pile them high with cold cuts, cheese, tomatoes, sweet commercial mayonnaise, and sometimes mustard, too. Pickles and even ketchup might top the pile. Indeed there is quite a cornucopia of flavor packed into our standard "deli sandwich."

My kids will settle for nothing less. But they don't drink wine with their lunch, and I do. A glass of wine at lunch hardly slows me down for the afternoon. It does, however, transform a sandwich into a dining experience. Consider the option of simplicity and purity of flavor between two slices of bread. That's the best complement for a glass of fine rosé.

To the French, *jambon et beurre* (ham and butter) on a crusty, fresh baguette is what ham and cheese is to Americans. It's standard fare. The salty, sweet ham flavors are carried along the palate by the butter, which also moistens the bread. Ham and cheese is also enjoyed with additional butter throughout southern France.

Prosciutto is so flavorful on its own, it needs nothing more than a touch of butter as a sandwich foil. As an alternative, try Italian *soppressata,* or any thin-sliced dry-cured French sausage, such as *saucisson.* The meat should never be thickly layered. It's the crusty, fresh bread and sweet butter that provide substance here. Think of the meat as garnish.

2 ounces thinly sliced prosciutto (about 4 slices)
1/2 to 1 tablespoon unsalted butter
1/2 fresh baguette (6 to 10 inches long)

- Cut the baguette in half lengthwise and spread the butter evenly across one of the bread halves. Loosely drape the prosciutto slices over the butter. Seal with the top half of the baguette.

serves 1

fish soup WITH AIOLI

Why we don't eat more fish soup in America is a mystery to me. In southern France, this heartwarming, savory dish is more popular than chicken soup, and it's really easy to make, too. Don't be frightened by the long list of ingredients. Most of them are simply thrown in the pot, boiled, and then strained. If you're using a whole fish, don't worry about removing the gills, as most cookbooks advise. I haven't found they add bitterness, despite beliefs to the contrary.

Aioli, or garlic mayonnaise, adds richness and body to the soup. French diners will add saffron and hot peppers to an aioli to make a rouille, which is then added to the soup along with crunchy toast croutons. I've toned down the heat, kept the saffron in the soup (not in the aioli), and made the croutons optional.

2 tablespoons olive oil

2 onions, sliced

3 carrots, peeled and coarsely chopped

3 celery stalks, coarsely chopped

1 white-fleshed fish (3 to 4 pounds) such as cod, flounder, or halibut,
    scaled and gutted (with or without head and tail)

1/2 teaspoon dried thyme, 1 bay leaf, 2 to 4 sprigs fresh flat-leaf parsley, and
    2 sprigs fresh tarragon, tied in a cheesecloth square to make a bouquet garni

1 large head garlic, halved

2 tablespoons tomato paste

2 1/2 pounds fresh, ripe tomatoes, chopped, or 28 ounces canned whole
    Italian (plum) tomatoes, with juice

1 teaspoon saffron threads

1/4 teaspoon cayenne pepper

1 large potato, peeled and coarsely chopped

1 teaspoon sea salt, plus more to taste

Freshly ground black pepper

1 cup toasted bread croutons (optional)

1 1/2 cups Aioli (page 83)

Crusty bread for serving (optional)

- In a large saucepan or a soup pot, heat the olive oil over medium heat. Add the onions, carrots, and celery and sauté until moderately tender, about 5 minutes. Add the fish (cut in pieces, if necessary, to fit into the pan) and cook, turning frequently, until the flesh begins to fall off the bones, about 10 minutes.

- Add the bouquet garni, garlic, tomato paste, tomatoes, saffron, cayenne, potato, and 1 teaspoon salt to the pan. Add water to cover the contents. Bring to a boil, reduce the heat to a simmer, cover, and cook until the potato is tender, about 45 minutes.

- Remove the bouquet garni and coarsely purée the soup in a blender or food processor. Strain the purée through a fine-mesh sieve or colander, forcing the liquid through with the back of a large spoon. Discard all solids.

- To serve, gently reheat the soup to a simmer. Ladle it into individual serving bowls. Season to taste with salt and black pepper. Add 3 to 5 croutons (if using) to each bowl and top each portion with a dollop or two of the Aioli. Serve with crusty bread (if desired) and a bottle of chilled rosé.

serves 4 to 6 as a first course

fried oysters

The French deserve a lot of credit for their culture of fine dining and rosé. But sometimes, because of their strong traditions, they miss out on a good thing. Oysters and rosé are an example.

I was once sitting at a seaside oyster bar in the port town of Bandol, south of Marseille, where I ordered a shimmering plate of raw oysters. Looking at the wine list, I decided to order one of the tangy, bright-edged local rosés. But my French friends protested, telling me it was "white wine, bubbly, or bust," where oysters were concerned.

Ignoring this Franco-babble, I ordered the rosé anyway. Ultimately, we all agreed that the lemony, mineral qualities in the light pink wine matched up beautifully with the briny, mineral flavors in the oysters.

At home, try the following recipe for fried oysters, which also pair marvelously with rosé. I use jarred fresh-shucked Pacific or Atlantic oysters, which are widely available in specialty food and fish markets around the country and spare you the trouble of shucking the oysters. The oysters are fried in chile-laced cornmeal, which gives them extra zing and a special affinity for a refreshingly fruit-laced quaff.

Canola oil for deep-frying

3 cups cornmeal

2 teaspoons chipotle chile flakes or red pepper flakes

2 teaspoons salt

1 jar (1 quart) fresh-shucked oysters (about 30 medium-sized oysters)

Juice of 2 or 3 lemons

- Pour the canola oil to a depth of 1 inch into a deep, heavy, large sauté pan or skillet and heat over medium-high heat until it begins to bubble slightly. Meanwhile, in a bowl, stir together the cornmeal, chile flakes, and salt.

(CONTINUED)

- Reduce the heat to medium. Quickly dredge the oysters—2 to 4 at a time—in the cornmeal mixture and immediately place them in the hot oil. (If necessary, reduce the heat to prevent the oil from splattering and smoking.) Repeat until the pan is filled with oysters. Depending on the size of your oysters and pan, you should be able to fry 8 to 12 oysters at once.

- Using tongs, a slotted spoon, or wooden chopsticks, carefully turn the oysters when they become golden brown at their edges, after 2 to 3 minutes. The second side will cook more quickly than the first side, within 1 to 2 minutes. Be careful not overcook the oysters or they will dry out. They should remain moist and plump inside their golden, crisp cornmeal crust.

- Using the tongs, spoon, or chopsticks, transfer the oysters to a serving plate lined with paper towels. Drizzle with some of the lemon juice and serve immediately. Fry the remaining oysters in 2 or 3 batches.

serves 4

seafood aioli

Throughout France, Spain, and Italy, the garlic mayonnaise known as aioli is enjoyed as a condiment for many different foods. Diners typically place a dollop of aioli on their plates and dip whatever they are eating into the smooth, creamy, tangy sauce. Here, aioli pairs equally well with fish and steamed vegetables.

Despite the multiple steps listed below, this seafood aioli is quite simple to prepare. You could simplify it even more by using a high-quality commercial mayonnaise. But commercial mayonnaise is usually sweetened and doesn't taste like a true aioli. Fortunately, homemade mayonnaise is remarkably easy to prepare, and it's worth taking an extra 5 minutes to do so.

Remember that homemade mayonnaise is made with raw eggs. This fact makes the threat of salmonella poisoning a real—if highly unlikely—one, particularly for small children, pregnant women, older individuals, or anyone with a compromised immune system. If you have concerns regarding salmonella, buy a good commercial mayonnaise that relies less on sugar and more on fine ingredients for flavor. That said, my family has always enjoyed homemade mayonnaise without incident. Use fresh eggs from a reputable source for the best results.

This seafood aioli makes a striking, colorful tabletop presentation that's easy enough to prepare and enjoy on weeknights. But it is also excellent for a weekend dinner party. You may select whatever fish looks freshest at the market, although meaty fish like salmon, swordfish, and tuna work particularly well.

Of course, a backdrop of crisp, refreshing rosé completes the picture. Top your table with a bottle or two.

6 red potatoes, about 3 pounds total weight, unpeeled, scrubbed and quartered

4 carrots, about 1½ pounds total weight, peeled and cut into 2-inch lengths

1 pound string beans, trimmed

Salt and freshly ground pepper

2 pounds fish steaks such as salmon, halibut, or swordfish, about 1½ inches thick

2 teaspoons extra-virgin olive oil

1½ cups Aioli (recipe follows)

(CONTINUED)

- Prepare a fire in a charcoal grill or preheat a gas grill to medium.

- Bring a saucepan three-fourths full of water to a boil, add the potatoes and carrots, and cook until tender, about 15 minutes. Drain in a colander and cover to keep warm.

- While the potatoes and carrots are cooking, in another saucepan, steam the string beans in a steamer basket set over 1 inch of boiling water or boil them in water to cover until tender, 6 to 8 minutes. Drain and cover to keep warm.

- Lightly salt and pepper the fish on both sides, then brush on both sides with the olive oil. Place on the grill rack and grill, turning once, until opaque throughout, 4 to 5 minutes per side. Remove from the grill and cut into serving pieces.

- To serve, arrange the vegetables, grouped separately, on a large serving platter. Place the fish on a separate platter and the aioli in a serving bowl. Diners can help themselves as desired.

AIOLI

Aioli is a simple garlic mayonnaise used in many dishes throughout the Mediterranean.

1 egg yolk, at room temperature

1 teaspoon Dijon mustard

Salt

1/2 cup extra-virgin olive oil

1/2 cup canola oil

1 clove garlic, minced

- In a bowl, combine the egg yolk, mustard, and salt to taste and whisk to blend. Whisk in the oils, a very small amount at a time, until an emulsified sauce forms. Alternatively, in a food processor or blender, pulse the egg yolk, mustard, and salt to combine. With the machine running, add the oils in a fine, steady stream, processing until an emulsified sauce forms. Stir the garlic into the mayonnaise. Taste and adjust the salt if needed.

serves 4 to 6 | AIOLI: makes about 1 1/2 cups

pâtes au pistou (PASTA WITH BASIL PESTO)

In the United States, most people think of fresh basil pesto as an Italian specialty. But pesto is considered a regional treasure in Nice, on France's Côte d'Azur, where the locals call it *pistou*. Ideal for pasta, it can also be served on tomato salads, in sandwiches, and with numerous other dishes. The French even make a *soupe au pistou*. This fresh herb sauce is, of course, a natural partner for rosé.

For this pasta dish, be careful not to use too much *pistou*. Start with a dollop, toss, taste, and add more if desired. Use either fresh or dried pasta. Any shape will do.

Pine nuts are a traditional ingredient that weaves a hint of tangy sweetness into the sauce. Sometimes walnuts are used instead. But if you don't have any nuts on hand, the sauce can still taste quite good, blended with nutty, freshly grated Parmesan cheese. *Pistou* can be stored in the refrigerator for several days.

3/4 to 1 cup extra-virgin olive oil

4 cups firmly packed fresh basil leaves

2 tablespoons pine nuts (optional)

1/2 cup freshly grated Parmesan cheese, plus extra for serving (optional)

2 cloves garlic, minced

Salt and freshly ground pepper

1 pound dried pasta or 1 1/2 pounds fresh pasta (any shape)

- In a blender or food processor, combine 1/4 cup of the olive oil and the basil leaves and process until puréed, adding additional oil in 1/4-cup increments as needed to achieve a smooth consistency. Add the pine nuts (if using) and the 1/2 cup Parmesan and continue to process until smooth. Add the garlic and pulse until it is incorporated. If the pistou is still too thick after all the olive oil is added, add a few more tablespoons, one tablespoon at a time, until the desired consistency is reached. Season to taste with salt and pepper. Transfer to a serving bowl and set aside.

(CONTINUED)

- In a large pot, bring 4 quarts lightly salted water to a boil over high heat. Add the pasta all at once and stir it a bit as it softens. Reduce the heat slightly, but keep it high enough to maintain a boil without splattering the stove. When the pasta is no longer crunchy, but still firm and chewy (about 10 minutes for dried pasta, 3 minutes for fresh pasta), drain it in a colander and shake dry. Do not rinse it with water or the pistou will not adhere well to the noodles.

- Divide the pasta among individual plates or bowls. Allow each diner to garnish his or her pasta with pistou to taste. They can then toss their own pâtes au pistou using a fork and knife. Garnish with additional pistou, Parmesan (if desired), salt, and pepper to taste.

serves 4 or 5

braised lamb <small>WITH INDIAN SPICES</small>

Rosé may not be an integral part of India's deliciously intriguing culinary tradition, but it pairs beautifully with the aromas and accents of the East. Today, many Indian restaurants around the country present wine lists—some better than others. More often than not, these wine selections rarely offer patrons the same quality and interest as the dishes on the menu.

It seems that America's love affair with red wine has placed undo emphasis on the category where it is least appropriate. Often tannic and generally served too warm, red wines such as Cabernet Sauvignon or Merlot top the wine lists at many Indian restaurants. They clash mightily with the robust, exotic herbs and spices in most Indian food. Fresh, fruity Zinfandel would make a better red wine selection for some dishes, but I prefer lighter-styled rosé for this culinary arena.

I also see plenty of richly textured, well-oaked Chardonnay on Indian restaurant wine lists. But again, that's not my first choice for chicken tandoori or a spiced lamb stew such as the one featured in the recipe below.

And what about beer with Indian cuisine? Well, I love it. But in my opinion, beer is a marvelous thirst-quencher that rightly plays second fiddle to a well-chosen wine as a mealtime beverage.

What continues to surprise me about most Indian restaurant wine lists is the scarcity of rosé. Usually, I find none at all. Sometimes I'll find a sweet White Zinfandel—hardly a candidate to accompany serious eating.

As you dine on the sublime spices of India and its neighboring cultures, and the heat in your dish is transferred to your brow, remember there is no better companion than cool, refreshing, dry rosé.

3 tablespoons canola or other vegetable oil

1¼ pounds boneless stewing lamb, cut into 1-inch cubes

3 onions, diced

1 tablespoon peeled and grated fresh ginger

2 cloves garlic, minced

2 tablespoons ground coriander

1 tablespoon paprika

(CONTINUED)

$^1/_2$ teaspoon cayenne pepper

$^1/_4$ cup plain yogurt

2 tomatoes, diced

1 cup water

1$^1/_2$ teaspoons salt, plus more to taste

1 pound fresh spinach, tough stems removed

$^1/_2$ cup chopped fresh cilantro

Freshly ground black pepper

- In a Dutch oven or other large, heavy pot, heat 2 tablespoons of the oil over medium-high heat. Add the lamb cubes and sear on all sides, about 5 minutes. Transfer the lamb to a plate and set aside.

- Add the remaining 1 tablespoon oil to the pot and reduce the heat to medium. Add the onions and sauté until translucent, about 3 minutes. Stir in the ginger, garlic, coriander, paprika, cayenne, and yogurt. Reduce the heat to low and simmer, uncovered, for 3 to 4 minutes. Return the meat to the pot and add the tomatoes, water, and the 1$^1/_2$ teaspoons salt. Raise the heat to medium high and bring to a boil. Cover, reduce the heat to low, and cook until the meat is very tender, about 1 hour.

- When the meat is nearly done, rinse the spinach and steam in a sauté pan with just the water clinging to the leaves until wilted, 2 to 3 minutes. Drain and coarsely chop.

- Stir the chopped spinach and cilantro into the stew and simmer, uncovered, for another 5 minutes. Taste and adjust the seasoning with salt and black pepper, then serve.

serves 4 to 6

braised rabbit WITH TOMATOES, FRESH SAGE, AND POLENTA

Located in the heart of Napa Valley, Tra Vigne is a restaurant that has long celebrated the seamless marriage of Italian and northern California cooking traditions. Diners enjoy pure and elegant flavors anchored in the fundamentals of olive oil and herbs, which frame the seasonal bounty featured on the daily menu.

While many local vintners can proudly point to their own red and white wines on the wine list, Tra Vigne's dining selections are also deliriously well suited to dry rosé, particularly during lunch in the garden patio.

This dish, developed by executive chef Michael Reardon, serves up a savory blend of tender, bite-sized rabbit morsels couched in a sage-infused sauce that tops the cornmeal porridge known as polenta. The recipe also calls for 2 cups of dry rosé. However, a dry white or red cooking wine will also work in the sauce.

FOR THE RABBIT:

2 or 3 large ripe tomatoes, peeled, or 14 ounces canned whole Italian
    (plum) tomatoes, with juice

2 tablespoons extra-virgin olive oil

2 medium onions, cut into small dice

1 celery stalk, cut into small dice

2 medium carrots, peeled and cut into small dice

3 bay leaves

3 sprigs fresh sage (6 to 8 leaves on each)

10 medium cloves garlic, peeled

2 cups dry rosé wine

1 rabbit (3 to 4 pounds)

Salt and freshly ground pepper

4 cups chicken stock or canned low-sodium broth

(CONTINUED)

FOR THE POLENTA:

4 cups water

1 teaspoon salt

1 cup polenta (not instant)

1/2 cup half-and-half or heavy cream

2 tablespoons unsalted butter

1/2 cup freshly grated Parmesan cheese, plus extra for serving (optional)

TO MAKE THE RABBIT:

- In a blender or food processor, pulse the tomatoes to a coarse purée and set aside. Heat the olive oil in a large, deep-sided sauté pan over medium-high heat. Add the onions, celery, and carrots and sauté until the onions are partially translucent, stirring occasionally to prevent burning, 7 to 10 minutes. Stir in the bay leaves, 1 sprig of the sage, and the garlic cloves. Add the wine and 1 cup of the tomato purée. (You may have a little purée left, which can be saved for another use or discarded.) Simmer, uncovered, over medium-high heat, stirring occasionally, until most of the liquid has evaporated, about 15 minutes.

- While the sauce simmers, remove the rabbit's legs at the joints and cut the body in half or into pieces that will fit into the sauté pan. Lightly salt and pepper the meat.

- Add the rabbit pieces and the chicken stock to the sauce. Spoon the liquid over any parts of the rabbit not completely submerged. Bring the liquid to a boil, reduce heat to medium low, cover, and simmer until the rabbit is cooked through, about 35 minutes.

- Using a slotted spoon, transfer the rabbit pieces to a large platter and let stand until cool enough to handle, about 10 minutes. Meanwhile, raise the heat under the pan to medium high and simmer the sauce, uncovered, until reduced by half, about 20 minutes. Taste and adjust the seasoning.

- While the sauce is simmering, remove the leaves from the remaining 2 sage sprigs. Coarsely chop and set them aside. Discard the stalks. When the rabbit is cool, pull the meat off the bones and into bite-sized pieces. (Use a knife to trim stubborn bits of meat.) Reserve in a bowl.

- Remove the sage sprig and bay leaves from the sauce and discard. Stir the chopped sage and the rabbit pieces into the sauce and simmer for 5 more minutes. Adjust the seasoning with additional salt and pepper to taste. Cover to keep warm while making the polenta.

TO MAKE THE POLENTA:

- Combine the water and salt in a 3- or 4-quart saucepan and bring to a boil. Slowly whisk in the polenta, then reduce the heat until the polenta gently bubbles. Stir in the half-and-half and continue to simmer, stirring occasionally with a wooden spoon as the polenta thickens.

- After about 10 minutes, all the liquid should be absorbed and the polenta should have a smooth consistency. Remove from the heat. Add the butter and $1/2$ cup Parmesan and stir until both have melted into the polenta. Pour into a high-sided platter or baking dish and allow it to settle for a few minutes to firm up.

- To serve, gently reheat the rabbit if necessary. (It should be quite hot.) Spoon a serving of polenta onto individual plates and top with the rabbit sauce. Lightly garnish with additional freshly grated Parmesan cheese, if desired.

serves 4 or 5

chicken couscous

Once, while sitting in a small Tunisian restaurant near the old port in Marseille, France, I was contemplating all sorts of marvelous North African specialties on the menu. But in the end I couldn't pass up the house couscous, which came brimming with great chunks of lamb, *merguez* sausages, and poultry. It was served over a mound of moist, fine couscous grains, which deftly soaked up the sauce.

Spicy *harissa* (a condiment made with ground peppers, cayenne, cumin, and coriander) added heat to the dish, and I reached for a sip of cool, refreshing Algerian rosé to quench my thirst. As far as food and wine pairings go, it was pretty near perfect.

Considering that alcoholic beverages are forbidden in traditional Muslim society, it's surprising to think that wine is still produced in Algeria, Tunisia, and Morocco. The North African wine industry is a vestige of these countries' colonial history with France.

In the past, robust North African wines typically were used to beef up the blends of many French wines. Not surprisingly, North African wine production has decreased measurably since the end of the colonial era. In a sign of even drier times to come, the Algerian government passed a law in 2003 banning the importation of all alcoholic beverages. The ruling may give local wineries a monopoly on sales, but it will hardly create an environment conducive to making great wine. Nonetheless, the Coteaux de Mascara Algerian rosé that I enjoyed in Marseille was light, fresh, and clean tasting.

Technically speaking, couscous is actually a grainlike pasta made with semolina or barley. The following recipe features chicken framed in the exotic flavors of North Africa. It will match well with any of your favorite pink wines—bubbly included. Look for *harissa*, which comes as a prepared paste in a tube or a can, in specialty food shops and fine supermarkets. To save time in the kitchen, ask your butcher to cut the chicken into 8 to 10 pieces in what is sometimes called a "fricassee cut."

(CONTINUED)

1 tablespoon cumin seeds

1 tablespoon coriander seeds

2 pinches saffron threads

3 whole cinnamon sticks

1/8 teaspoon cayenne pepper

1 small bunch cilantro (about 20 sprigs)

1/4 cup extra-virgin olive oil

2 large onions, coarsely chopped

5 large cloves garlic, minced

1 piece fresh ginger root (about 1 1/2 inches long), peeled and finely chopped

4 plum tomatoes, quartered (but not peeled or seeded)

1 roasting chicken (about 5 pounds), skin intact, cut into 8 to 10 pieces

3 teaspoons salt

1/2 teaspoon freshly ground pepper

Three 14-ounce cans (42 ounces) low-sodium chicken broth

2 cups water

2 cups instant couscous

1 pound large carrots, peeled and cut into 1-inch-long round segments

1 large fresh fennel bulb, stalks removed, sliced lengthwise into eighths (optional)

1 1/2 pounds small zucchini, ends trimmed and cut into 2-inch-long round segments

One 15-ounce can chickpeas

Harissa to taste (see recipe introduction)

- In a small, dry skillet over medium heat, toast the cumin seeds, stirring constantly, until fragrant, 2 to 3 minutes. Transfer to a flat cutting surface and, using the flat edge of a wide-bladed knife, crush the seeds into a coarse powder. Set aside in a small bowl.

- Repeat the same toasting and crushing process with the coriander seeds. Then place them in the bowl with the cumin and stir to blend. Place the saffron on top of the seed mixture. Place the cinnamon sticks and cayenne in the spice bowl as well and set aside.

- Roughly chop the cilantro—both leaves and stems—and set aside.

- In a large pot, heat the olive oil over high heat. Add the onions and sauté, stirring occasionally to prevent burning, until translucent, about 2 minutes. Add the garlic and stir occasionally for 1 minute. Add the ginger and cook for 1 minute. Stir in the tomatoes. Stir in the spice mixture. Add the chicken pieces and stir to coat well. Stir in the cilantro, 2 teaspoons of the salt, and the pepper. Add the chicken broth, cover, and bring to a boil. Reduce the heat to simmer and cook, covered, for 30 minutes.

- While the chicken is cooking, prepare the couscous. In a saucepan, combine the water and the remaining 1 teaspoon salt and bring to a boil. Remove from the heat and, using a fork, stir in the couscous. Cover and let stand until the water is absorbed and the couscous is tender, 5 to 10 minutes. Uncover and fluff the couscous with the fork. Cover again and set aside until ready to serve.

- When the chicken has simmered for 30 minutes, add the carrots and the fennel, if using. Cover and simmer for 20 more minutes. Add the zucchini, cover again, and simmer for 10 more minutes. Add the chickpeas, cover, and simmer for 5 more minutes.

- To serve, spoon about 1/2 cup of the cooked couscous into each of 6 individual bowls. Ladle the chicken and vegetable stew over the couscous. In a small bowl, combine 1/2 cup of liquid from the stew and *harissa* to taste and stir to dissolve. Each diner can then garnish his or her own dish with *harissa* sauce, depending on the desired level of heat.

serves 6

pork tenderloin WITH ANCHO CHILE SAUCE, RED BEANS AND RICE, FRIED PLANTAINS, AND AVOCADO SALAD

Most people think Mexican food is meant to be enjoyed with a cold beer. (If you're drinking margaritas with your meal, think again. A margarita is really a tequila "milkshake," best enjoyed on its own.)

Actually, beer *is* a pretty good match for Mexican-inspired dishes. But really fine Mexican cooking is brimming with complex flavors that scream out for more finesse in the beverage department. Rosé is blessed with a fruit-driven, bright-edged core that blends well with the fiery, ripe fruit found in chiles. Refreshingly chilled, dry, pink wine also cools down the palate.

This set of recipes offers a full meal of Mexican-accented food. The thick ancho chile sauce is a lush and only slightly spicy component. (Look for dried ancho chiles in specialty food shops and many fine grocery stores.)

Rice and beans are traditionally served on the side. The sweet, earthy flavors of fried, ripe, bananalike plantains add additional interest. Finally, a simple platter of sliced avocado dressed with onion and lemon juice adds a creamy-smooth contrast.

Serve the ancho pork, beans and rice, plaintains, and avocado salad on separate large platters. Diners can then help themselves to a portion of each and enjoy in various combinations.

1 teaspoon cumin seeds

5 dried ancho chiles

3 tablespoons canola oil

1 large onion, sliced

3 large cloves garlic, sliced

One 14-ounce can low-sodium chicken broth

1 teaspoon salt

1 pound pork tenderloin, cut into thin strips

Red Beans and Rice (page 100)

Fried Plantains (page 101)

Avocado Salad (page 101)

- In a small, dry skillet over medium heat, toast the cumin seeds, stirring constantly, until fragrant, 2 to 3 minutes. Set them aside in a small bowl.

- Using the same pan, raise the heat to high and press each chile onto the hot surface, first on one side and then on another, to sear for about 30 seconds per side. (This "wakes up" the chiles, making them more fragrant.) Let them cool for a minute and then, using your hands, pull them apart enough to empty them of their seeds. Discard the seeds and stems. Place the chiles in a bowl and fill with water to cover. Set aside to soak.

- In a large sauté pan, heat 1 tablespoon of the oil over medium heat. Add the onion and cook until lightly browned, stirring occasionally to prevent burning, about 4 minutes. Stir in the garlic and toasted cumin seeds and sauté for 2 more minutes, stirring occasionally.

- Drain the chiles and add them to the pan, stirring for about 1 minute. Transfer the onion mixture to a blender. Add the broth and blend to a smooth purée. Transfer the purée to a saucepan, add the salt, and bring to a simmer. Add more salt to taste if desired. Turn off the heat, cover the pan, and set aside.

- In a large skillet, heat the remaining 2 tablespoons oil over high heat. Add the pork, stirring occasionally to keep it from sticking, and cook until browned on all sides, about 3 minutes. Pour the chile sauce over the meat, reduce the heat to medium, and cook for 1 more minute. Transfer to a serving platter. To serve, pass at the table along with platters of red beans and rice, fried plantains, and avocado salad.

serves 6 to 8

(CONTINUED)

RED BEANS AND RICE

With all the different steps involved in this section, I'd simply use two 15-ounce cans of kidney beans. But if you want to cook your dried red beans from scratch, make them before starting any of the other recipes in this section, using one of the methods below.

> 2 cups dried red or pink kidney beans
>
> Water to cover beans, plus 2 cups water or canned low-sodium chicken
> broth for rice
>
> 2 1/2 teaspoons salt
>
> 1 cup long- or short-grain white rice

LONG-SOAK METHOD:

- Rinse and pick over the beans. Soak them overnight in water to cover by 2 inches. Drain. In a large pot, add cold water to cover again by 2 inches. Bring to a boil, add 2 teaspoons of the salt, and reduce the heat to a simmer. Cook, covered, until tender, 45 minutes to an hour. Drain the beans in a colander and keep warm until ready to serve.

QUICK-SOAK METHOD:

- In a large pot, bring 8 cups water to a boil. Add 2 teaspoons of the salt, then add the beans and cover. Return to a boil and cook for 5 minutes. Remove from the heat and let the beans soak for 1 to 1 1/2 hours. Drain the beans in a colander. Return them to the pot, cover with water by 2 inches, and bring to a boil. Reduce the heat to a simmer and cook, uncovered, until tender, 30 to 45 minutes. Drain the beans in a colander and keep warm until ready to serve.

- Meanwhile, in a saucepan, bring the 2 cups water to a boil and add the remaining 1/2 teaspoon salt. Stir in the rice, return to a boil, then cover, reduce the heat to low, and cook until all the water has been absorbed, 15 to 20 minutes. Keep warm until ready to serve.

FRIED PLANTAINS

1 cup canola oil or safflower oil
3 ripe plantains, peeled and cut into $1/2$-inch-thick slices
Coarse sea salt or kosher salt

- In a large, deep skillet or sauté pan, heat the oil over medium-high heat. Place the plantain slices in the hot oil and cook until golden brown on both sides, about 10 minutes. Flip the slices occasionally so they brown evenly.

- Using a slotted spoon, transfer the plantains to paper towels to drain. Sprinkle lightly with salt.

AVOCADO SALAD

2 large avocados
$1/2$ onion, thinly sliced into rounds
Juice of 1 lemon
Coarse sea salt or kosher salt

- Cut the avocados in half and remove the large pits. Lay the halves, cut side down, on a cutting board, and cut lengthwise into slices $1/4$ to $1/2$ inch thick. Peel the skin off each slice and lay the skinned slices on a serving plate.

- Garnish the avocado with the onion slices and drizzle with the lemon juice. Season with the salt.

RED BEANS AND RICE; FRIED PLANTAINS; AVOCADO SALAD: serves 6 to 8

7 a tasting guide

TO ROSÉS FROM AROUND
THE WORLD

When I counted over two hundred fifty local rosés on display at a supermarket in the French city of Aix-en-Provence, I realized that a listing here could never come close to being comprehensive from a French or a world perspective. There are just too many producers, many of whom do not even export. And with newcomers appearing each vintage—from both Europe and the New World—it's virtually impossible to keep up with them all.

But discovery is one of the great joys of wine drinking. The players change, methods evolve, and vintage quality fluctuates. No year is exactly the same, and winemakers will always make wines that reflect the ups and downs of the growing season.

Look for consistency of style among wineries, but expect and welcome variations on the theme.

Vintages are not listed in the following chart because the research, production, and publication of this book spanned several vintage releases. Instead, the wine descriptions in this guide are designed to give the reader an idea of what to expect from a given winery in terms of style. A wine may be brightly textured, with zippy acidity and crisp mineral notes—a style that would pair well with shellfish or tangy olives. Or it may be more full-bodied and fruit-driven, making it a perfect match for burgers, pizza, grilled salmon, barbecue, or even a juicy steak.

You will notice that many of the wines share similar descriptive terms, such as "mineral" or "bright." Flavors repeatedly include such core elements as cherry and citrus. There is good reason for this: rosé could hardly be called a wine category if there were no common characteristics among the various bottles.

As with all wines, though, rosé is made in a wide range of styles. The list of wines and descriptions that follow are meant to help you determine what awaits behind the labels you may discover on your favorite wineshop's rosé shelf. Of course, there is really no substitute for tasting a wine. So let your own palate be the ultimate arbiter of good taste.

Prices change from year to year and state to state, so prices are not included here. Most rosé is either very reasonably priced or very expensive. At the lower end, you'll find, with only a few exceptions, mainly still wines (wines without bubbles). These wines can range in price from as little as five or six dollars to between fifteen and twenty dollars. Sometimes they cost a bit more.

The discrepancy in the price of wine, from five-dollar bottles to hallowed "cult wines" priced for the privileged at hundreds of dollars a bottle, is a perennial mystery to many nonexperts. The simplest explanation is that some wines cost more to produce than others. Grapes from famous wine regions such as California's Napa Valley or France's Bandol region may have a higher commercial value than grapes issuing from other areas. Cooperage, tanks, and other equipment can also affect production costs. Availability is also an issue. Sometimes only a small amount of a highly allocated wine is available, while other times thousands of cases flood the market. These are all conditions that can affect the price of any wine, rosé or otherwise.

What currently keeps the cost of rosé comparatively low is the market perception that it is a less-than-serious wine. Simple, sweet, inexpensive White Zinfandels and the like have shaped many Americans' perception of rosé. It may take some time for wine consumers to appreciate the fact that pink wines are also made in a drier, more complex, and food-friendlier style.

Even in France, where rosé is widely imbibed, it still doesn't get the same respect as many white or red wines. But, as they say, the cream rises to the top. Those rosés that merit special attention will generally cost more as supply affects demand. It's up to you, as an educated consumer, to decide whether the wine you are drinking is worth the price you've paid for it.

At the high end of the price spectrum lie certain sparkling rosés, particularly those from France's Champagne region. In Champagne, only about 3 percent of all wine production is pink. As somewhat of a rarity, Champagne rosé is valued at a higher price than many of the region's traditional sparkling wines, which are already fairly expensive.

Outside of Champagne, prices for pink wines made in the *méthode champenoise* (see page 60) tend to be lower, though they are usually higher than still wines. In contrast to the high-end French sparklers, Italian style *frizzante* (see page 63) is usually inexpensive, but quite delicious. It's sweet, but there is a time and place for a good sweet rosé, typically before a meal, as an aperitif.

As a rule, drink rosé in its youth, when it is fresh and lively. However, some of the more complex rosés age quite nicely over several years, revealing increased layers of fruit and flavor. Occasionally, rosé may be extremely ageworthy, like the 1954 Canto Perdrix from Tavel mentioned on page 22. In general, though, I recommend drinking rosé within a few years of its vintage date.

ROSÉ: A WORLD PERSPECTIVE

The following chart features an eclectic international selection of some two hundred rosés, both still and sparkling. Some are more widely distributed than others, but generally, at least a few should be available at your favorite wineshops and restaurants. If they are not, consider asking your local wine merchant or sommelier to include some in their next wine order.

With the exception of the sparkling wines, these rosés are grouped in alphabetical order by their country or state of origin. They are listed by their brand name first, followed by any other identifying names, and then their appellation, as it appears on the label. Sparkling wines are listed after the still wines, also by region of origin.

STILL WINE

ALGERIA

COTEAUX DE MASCARA

Clean, crisp, mild, and pleasant tasting, with hints of cherry, citrus, and spice.

AUSTRALIA

CHARLES MELTON | Barossa Valley

This is a big, full-bodied wine. Fairly dark in color, it shows a rich, black cherry center that gives way to hints of herb, anise, lemon, and grapefruit as well. A muscular rosé made for robust dining.

DOMINIQUE PORTET
Rosé Fontaine | Yarra Valley

Firm and focused, with bright citrus and mineral notes. Quite refreshing and interesting. Not surprisingly, it's made in a somewhat French style by a French expatriate.

GEOFF MERRILL | McLaren Vale

Typically a full-bodied, somewhat fleshy wine that features ripe cherry and strawberry fruit. It's solid and well structured, with good acidity for balance.

MARGAN
Hunter Valley | Shiraz Saignée

A big, meaty wine with a fine-tuned core of cherry, berry, and spice. Bright and fresh at the end.

PIZZINI | Rosetta | King Valley

Clean and bright, with pretty strawberry, cherry, herb, and spice notes. Moderate body.

PLANTAGENET
Eros | Western Australia

A dark-hued rosé—almost red—with a tannic edge framing pretty cherry and herb notes. Clean and firm on the finish.

WOODSTOCK
Free Run Grenache | McLaren Vale

A dark-colored, intensely cherry-like wine that's balanced by a touch of tannin and good acidity, serving up pleasing herbal notes on the finish.

YERING STATION
Pinot Noir Rosé | Yarra Valley

Crisp yet full-bodied, with a creamy-smooth texture and a fine-tuned mineral edge that's backed by cherry and citrus notes.

CALIFORNIA

ARROWOOD
La Rose | Sonoma Valley

An "off-dry" style that offers some sweetness with a strong cherry character. Try this as an aperitif.

BARON HERZOG | Zin Gris | Lodi

Well balanced and smooth on the palate, with lovely, subtle cherry and raspberry notes. Good body and moderate acidity give it staying power, though it finishes light and fresh.

BENESSERE
Rosato di Sangiovese | Napa Valley

Fairly lush, but with good structure, bright acidity, and fine cherry, citrus, mineral, and herb flavors. Lively at the end.

CAROL SHELTON
Rendezvous Rosé | North Coast

Kicks off with dark black cherry aromas, firm acidity, and fresh lemon and grapefruit flavors, which add interest and zip. Bright and clean on the finish. Made with Zinfandel, but bone-dry.

CHIMNEY ROCK
Rosé of Cabernet Franc |
Stags Leap District, Napa Valley

A dark-hued rosé with a cherry and herb core that's backed by bright acidity and a fresh, clean finish.

CUVAISON
Vin Gris | Carneros, Napa Valley

A dry, mineral-like style. Sleek and firm, with good acidity that's backed by hints of citrus, raspberry, and plum flavors.

EBERLE | Paso Robles

A smooth, silky textured wine that sports a bright cherry center. It's framed in raspberry, mineral, and citrus notes, finishing with moderate length.

ELYSE | Napa Valley

Quite floral in the nose, with subtle hints of pear and raspberry on the palate. It's fresh and lively at the end.

FETZER | Syrah Rosé | California

A full-bodied wine with rich cherry and raspberry notes at its core. Hints of anise and herbs add interest.

FETZER | Valley Oaks | California

Lighter in texture and style than Fetzer's Syrah rosé. This one's made from Pinot Noir and offers fresh cherry, citrus, and herb flavors.

FIFE | Redhead Rosé | Mendocino County

Named after Dennis Fife's redheaded wife, renowned wine author and educator Karen MacNeil. The wine offers a well-balanced core of cherry, raspberry, citrus, and herb notes, with a clean, bright finish.

GARGIULO
Rosato di Sangiovese | Napa Valley

A light-textured rosé. Fresh and crisp, and sporting pretty cherry, lemon, grapefruit, and herb flavors. Bright and clean on the finish.

GARRETSON WINE COMPANY
The Celeidh | Paso Robles

A full-bodied, richly textured wine offering dark cherry and raspberry flavors up front and backed by a touch of herbs and citrus. It's bright and edgy on the finish, ending with moderate length.

HEITZ | Grignolino | Napa Valley

A fresh, fruity style that serves up raspberry, cherry, herb, and lemon notes.

HESS COLLECTION
Syrah Rosé | Monterey

Tightly wound, with zippy acidity. This wine blends its cherry core with lemony mineral tones to make a complex quaff.

HUNDRED ACRE | Napa Valley

A full-bodied, lush, and extraordinarily rich rosé, made in very small quantities by Hundred Acre winery. The wine is redolent of spice, plum, cherry, raspberry, chocolate, blackberry, ginger, and herbs. Dark-hued and muscular, it's a power-house among pinks.

IRON HORSE
Rosato di Sangiovese | Alexander Valley

Fresh, round, and light on the palate. Crisp and clean, with a mineral/lemon edge at the end.

IRON HORSE
Rosé de Pinot Noir | Green Valley

A bit leaner and more mineral-like than the winery's Rosato di Sangiovese.

JOLIESSE | Shiraz Rosé | California

A robust style, full-bodied and bright, with hints of cherry, cinnamon, and earth.

KOSTA-BROWN | Russian River Valley

Fresh, round, and elegant, this wine is made with Pinot Noir and shows off a pretty core of cherry and raspberry flavors, couched in sleek citrus and herb notes for added interest.

KULETO | Napa Valley

A delicate, light-textured rosé made with Sangiovese. It's fresh, crisp, and light to the end.

L'UVAGGIO DI GIACOMO
Barbera Rosato | California

An elegant style that presents subtle cherry, herb, berry, citrus, and mineral flavors, ending with a fresh finish.

LA GRENOUILLE ROUGANTE
Napa Valley

Quite cherry-like at its core, but balanced by good, fresh acidity and a lemony twist at the end. From the folks at Frogs Leap.

LANG & REED | Wild Hare | Napa Valley

Typically made from Cabernet Franc, this lively little wine serves up a fine

blend of bing cherry, raspberry, citrus, and mineral flavors, all couched in medium body with a fresh finish.

LE PETIT PAGE | Napa Valley

Pretty, though somewhat muscular, with fruity cherry and strawberry notes.

MCDOWELL
Grenache | Mendocino County

This longtime producer makes a clean, fresh, fruity wine that offers pretty cherry and herb flavors backed by pleasing citrus notes.

MINER FAMILY
Mendocino Rosato | Mendocino

A lush, lively wine with complex raspberry, cherry, and strawberry flavors. Good acidity keeps it fresh and well balanced.

NORMAN VINEYARDS
Vino Rosado | Paso Robles

Quite light and fresh, with a pretty core of citrus, floral, and bing cherry notes.

THE OJAI VINEYARD
Vin du Soleil | California

A focused style that shows an interesting blend of herb, cherry, citrus, and raspberry flavors couched in firm acidity with a touch of tannin.

PEJU | Provence | Napa Valley

A fairly dark-hued rosé that's made with both red and white wines. Smooth in style, with cherry and raspberry notes at the fore.

PIPESTONE
Grenache Rosé | Paso Robles

Full-bodied and richly textured, with a smooth, black cherry and raspberry core that's followed by hints of spice and toast on the finish. A muscular rosé.

PRESTON OF DRY CREEK
Vin Gris | Dry Creek Valley

Crisp and light, with a pretty floral, raspberry, citrus center. Fresh and clean on the finish.

PRIMAROSA | SoloRosa | California

This special selection from SoloRosa highlights unusual characteristics found in a small number of barrels culled from each vintage. Production and distribution are extremely limited.

QUIVIRA
Wine Creek Ranch | Dry Creek Valley

Firm and focused, with pretty cherry, strawberry, citrus, mineral, and herb flavors. It remains clean and fresh on the finish.

RENARD | California

A fresh-tasting yet ample-bodied wine, redolent of bright cherry and supported by lovely lemon, anise, raspberry, and mineral flavors.

ROBERT HALL
Rosé de Robles | Paso Robles

With spicy cherry, anise, herb, and mineral notes at the fore, this medium-bodied wine has a fruity edge on the finish. A blend of Syrah, Grenache, and Mourvèdre.

ROBERT SINSKEY
Vin Gris of Pinot Noir | Los Carneros

Bright, fresh, and lemony, with plenty of floral and mineral notes. This pale pink wine initially evokes the style of Côtes de Provence, with its bright acidity and faint hue. But it's got California body that's balanced by a steely finish at the end.

RUTHERFORD HILL
Rosé of Merlot | Napa Valley

A full-bodied, creamy-textured wine that shows off pretty cherry, raspberry, herb, and citrus flavors at its core. It's fresh and bright to the end.

SAINTSBURY
Vincent Van Gris | Carneros

A well-balanced wine with firm acidity and pretty strawberry, raspberry, and citrus flavors. Made from Pinot Noir.

SAISON DES VINS
Le Printemps | Sonoma County

Despite what the name suggests, this wine is made in California. It's light-bodied and shows simple, fresh raspberry and cherry flavors with a hint of citrus at the end.

SANFORD
Pinot Noir Vin Gris | Santa Barbara County

A light-textured, elegant, and subtle wine that serves up cherry, rose petal, citrus, and mineral notes.

SAN MAURICE
Syrah Rosé | California

A medium-bodied wine that shows hints of cherry, peach, citrus, and herb flavors. The finish is fresh and lively.

SCHERRER WINERY
Vin Gris | Sonoma County

An elegant wine that still offers plenty of body, firm texture, and bright fruit flavors, including wild cherry, strawberry, minerals, and citrus notes. The wine is firm and clean on the finish.

SCOTT HARVEY
Rosé of Pinot Noir | Napa Valley

Well balanced, with a classy blend of fine-tuned acidity that supports a core of light cherry, raspberry, and citrus flavors. Sleek and elegant to the end.

SELBY | Sonoma County

This wine typically serves up cherry, strawberry, citrus, and herb flavors built around a core of good acidity. It's bright and clean on the finish.

SOLOROSA | California

Round-textured, with hints of cherry, raspberry, grapefruit, herb, and mineral notes. Full-bodied yet graced with bright acidity for balance and elegance, it finishes fresh and clean.

STOLPMAN | Santa Ynez Valley

Richly textured and broad on the palate, with hints of raspberry and strawberry, backed by mineral and herb flavors.

STORYBOOK MOUNTAIN
Zin Gris | Napa Valley

A dry pink Zinfandel that offers well-balanced cherry, raspberry, plum, and herb notes. A hint of grapefruit on the finish adds interest.

TABLAS CREEK VINEYARD | Paso Robles

A refreshing yet complex wine made from a blend of Mourvèdre, Grenache, and Counoise grapes—all Rhône varieties. It's got cherry, raspberry, and mineral flavors at its core, plus lemon, spice, and grapefruit through the finish.

TERRE ROUGE
Vin Gris d'Amador | Sierra Foothills

Light-textured and straightforward, this blend of Mourvèdre, Syrah, and Grenache offers modest raspberry, mineral, herb, and citrus flavors, all matched with finesse.

VALLEY OF THE MOON
Rosato di Sangiovese | Sonoma County

A full-bodied, ripe, darker styled wine that sports plenty of cherry and strawberry flavors, yet is dry and refreshing, with a hint of herbs on the finish.

VERDAD | Central Coast

A pretty wine, with pleasing strawberry, citrus, and cherry notes. It's got good, broad body and finishes with moderate length. From Bob and Louisa Lindquist, owners of Qupé.

VICTOR HUGO
Syrah Rosé | Paso Robles

A full-bodied style, dark in color and brimming with plenty of fruit flavors redolent of raspberry, strawberry, melon, and cherry. Quite intense, juicy, and fun.

VIN GRIS DE CIGARE
Pink Wine | California

A pleasing blend of tangy cherry, lemon, herb, and mineral flavors, couched in a light and refreshing style. From rosé pioneer Randall Grahm, of Bonny Doon.

VINUM CELLARS IT'S OK
Napa Valley

Very full-bodied and muscular. An unusually powerful wine for a rosé style,
it offers a lot of cherry and raspberry
flavors.

ZACA MESA | Z Gris | Santa Ynez Valley

A very fruity wine, still on the dry side,
but front-loaded with lots of cherry,
raspberry, and melony notes. Finishes
with a nice hint of citrus.

CHILE

COUSINO-MACUL | Gris

A pleasing wine with a strong mineral
edge that's deftly tempered with hints
of herb, raspberry, and citrus flavors.
Refreshing on the finish with a bright
note at the end.

FRANCE

ABARBANEL | White Shiraz | Pays L'Aude

The name implies that this wine would
be sweet and from Australia, where Syrah
is called Shiraz. However, it's French and
dry, with bright acidity and fresh grapefruit and cherry notes. Mineral-like on
the finish.

BÉLOUVÉ | Côtes de Provence

Light-textured and pale pink, this wine
serves up a blend of herbes de Provence,
backed with light raspberry and mineral
notes. Made by Domaines Bunan.

CANTO PERDRIX | Tavel

Quite bright, yet full-bodied with a
focused cherry, anise, and herb core
that fans out on the palate with a clean
citrus and mineral edge.

CHÂTEAU CAHUZAC | Fronton

A fine blend of black cherry, mineral,
and herb notes, couched in a focused,
silky texture. Clean and fresh on the end.

CHÂTEAU CALABRE | Bergerac Rosé

An elegant style that's well balanced,
showing a fine-tuned blend of ripe cherry,
raspberry, mineral, and citrus flavors.

CHÂTEAU CALISSANNE
Coteaux d'Aix-en-Provence

A round-textured style that's integrated
and elegant. It's got pretty raspberry,
cherry, grapefruit, and mineral flavors
and a fresh, clean finish.

CHÂTEAU D'ACQUERIA | Tavel

Full and richly textured, with cherry,
mineral, and citrus flavors. The wine is
fairly lush for a rosé, probably because
the winery leaves the grape skins in
contact with the juice longer than
many other producers.

CHÂTEAU DE BELLET | Alpes Maritimes

From Nice, this wine is pretty hard to
find but enjoys quite a reputation. Made
mostly with the obscure Braquet grape
(related to the Italian Brachetto). Full
on the palate, with hints of mandarin
orange, lemon, coffee, melon, spice,
and floral qualities, it's interesting and
unusual.

CHÂTEAU DE MANISSY
Auspice Clara | Tavel

A lovely nose, redolent of rose petals
and raspberries. It fans out to reveal
hints of earth, more floral notes, cherries,
and herbs. Bright on the finish.

CHÂTEAU DE PEYRASSOL
Cuvée Marie Estelle | Côtes de Provence

Bright and bracing, this light-hued wine
is made mostly from old-vine Mourvèdre
grapes and blended with a bit of Syrah.
It's got a serious dose of lemony grapefruit flavor that keeps it crisp and clean
to the very end. Very light in texture.

CHÂTEAU DE POURCIEUX
Côtes de Provence

Light-colored and smooth-textured, with
subtle hints of grapefruit, melon, cherry,
minerals, and lime. Bright on the finish.
A blend of Syrah, Grenache, and Cinsaut.

CHÂTEAU DE ROUËT
Cuvée Réservée | Côtes de Provence

Light and pleasant with bright citrus,
crab apple, and floral notes. Hints of
mineral and oranges show through on
the finish.

CHÂTEAU DE TRINQUEVEDEL | Tavel

Sleek and smooth, with a good cherry
core and an attractive earthy edge.
Bright lemon and mineral notes give
it grip, with a fresh, light finish.

CHÂTEAU FERRY-LACOMBE
Cuvée Lou Cascai | Trets-en-Provence

Fresh and light, with hints of lemon,
raspberry, herbs, and mineral notes.

CHÂTEAU FLANDREAU
Clairet | Bordeaux

Quite dark by rosé standards, this wine
serves up complex herbal notes backed
by hints of blackberry and cassis.

CHÂTEAU FONT DU BROC
Côtes de Provence

A trim, bright style. Quite lemony, and
also featuring pretty grapefruit, flint, and
herb flavors. Long and fresh on the finish.

CHÂTEAU LA BOUTIGNANE
Corbières

A light-textured wine with a strong
mineral and herb core. Behind it are
hints of cherries and citrus. Quite
refreshing.

CHÂTEAU LA ROUVIÈRE | Bandol

An elegant wine, with pretty citrus,
strawberry, cherry, and mineral flavors.
Smooth and sleek, with a long finish.
From Domaines Bunan.

CHÂTEAU MINUTY
Cuvée de L'Oratoire | Côtes de Provence

With its enticing aromas of flowers and
fruit, this lovely wine also offers complex hints of peach, melon, mineral, and
citrus flavors on the palate. It's got
great length and a clean, bright finish.

CHÂTEAU ROUBAUD
Cuvée Prestige | Costières de Nîmes

Bright cherry flavors are framed in pretty spice notes, finishing with a clean, mineral edge.

CHÂTEAU SAINTE ROSELINE
Cru Classé | Côtes de Provence

Very pale pink. Quite bright on the palate, with mineral-like, fresh, zingy lemon and grapefruit flavors. Comes in a distinctive bottle with a wide bottom and long graceful neck.

CLOS SAINTE MAGDELAINE | Cassis

Quite light in color, with subtle flavors that hint at watermelon, grapefruit, and orange peel. Elegant and refined.

CUVÉE PIERRE AUDONNET
Vin de Pays de Côtes Catalanes

This tasty wine from southwestern France reminds me of its nearby Spanish cousins. It's full, round, firm, smooth, and bright, with plenty of body and bright wild cherry, raspberry, citrus, mineral, and herb notes. Kind of a cross between Tavel and Rioja.

DOMAINE BRUNO CLAIR
Marsannay Rosé | Marsannay, Côte d'Or

A snappy, bright style of wine, strong in mineral and citrus flavors and steely on the finish.

DOMAINE CHARLES AUDOIN
Marsannay

Quite elegant, with lovely raspberry, citrus, herb, spice, and mineral notes. With good body and acidity, it's long and fresh on the finish.

DOMAINE DE FONTSAINTE
Gris de Gris | Corbières

A wine with impressive floral notes up front. Modest acidity makes it somewhat silky textured, with raspberry notes at the core.

DOMAINE DE L'HERMITAGE | Bandol

Quite bright and lean, with a strong citrus and mineral element that leaves the palate fresh and clean.

DOMAINE DE LA COURTADE
L'Alycastre | Côtes de Provence

A light-bodied wine that serves up a bright-edged bing cherry core. It's wrapped in zippy lemon and lime flavors, finishing squeaky clean.

DOMAINE DE LA JANASSE
Côtes du Rhône

Fairly rich on the palate, but with good acidity and freshness on the finish. Pretty cherry, mineral, and citrus flavors are at the core.

DOMAINE DE LA SAUVEUSE
Côtes de Provence

Light-colored and -textured, with bright lemon and grapefruit flavors. Mineral and herb notes abound on the fresh finish.

DOMAINE DE LA TOUR DU BON
Bandol

Light and fresh, with hints of strawberry, hay, citrus, and herbs. Clean on the finish with a bright edge.

DOMAINE DE NIZAS
Coteaux du Languedoc

Showing moderate body and brightness on the palate, this wine serves up a blend of cherry, citrus, spice, and herb flavors. Refreshing on the finish. From Bernard Portet, also of Clos du Val in Napa Valley.

DOMAINE DE SOUVIOU | Bandol

Light and fresh, with a pronounced citrus and mineral center. It's firm and bright and would go swimmingly with a fine bouillabaisse.

DOMAINE DES ROCHELLES
J.Y.A. Lebreton | Cabernet d'Anjou
Loire Valley

A pretty salmon color introduces this medium-bodied wine that offers pretty cherry and raspberry flavors supported by moderate acidity. It ends with a hint of lemon and mineral notes.

DOMAINE HOUCHART
Côtes de Provence

Crisp and lemony, with zippy grapefruit, herb, and melon notes. Clean and bright at the end.

DOMAINE LAFRAN-VEYROLLES
Bandol

Quite refined, with a well-integrated core of lemon, grapefruit, minerals, peach, toast, and herb flavors. The wine has medium body, finishing long and fresh.

DOMAINES OTT
Cuvée Marine | Bandol

Made in a lighter style, this wine offers good body nonetheless, and features a core of lemon, grapefruit, melon, mineral, and herb flavors. From the well-known estate that produces a number of distinctive bottlings.

DOMAINE SYLVAIN BAILLY
La Louée, La Croix Saint Ursin | Sancerre

Pale salmon in color and bright on the palate. Quite refreshing, with lemony notes up front. This is no fruit-driven wine, but rather a mineral-like rosé with a core of grapefruit and other citrus flavors. Bracing.

DOMAINE TEMPIER | Bandol

A famous name in rosé. Fresh and light, with a fine blend of mineral, citrus, melon, and spice notes. Vintage variation is quite noticeable in this wine. In warmer years, it is richer and lusher textured.

JEAN-LUC COLOMBO
Pioche et Cabanon Rosé |
Côte Bleue, Coteaux d'Aix en Provence

A pleasantly light-textured wine that offers bright-edged citrus, strawberry, and cherry flavors with a clean, fresh finish.

LA MORDORÉE | La Dame Rousse | Tavel

Fairly dark in color, with a solid cherry core. The wine has moderate body and sports flavors that are mineral and citrus-like in quality. Balanced and elegant.

LA VIEILLE FERME | Rhône Valley

Fairly straightforward and quite dry, this wine shows citrus and mineral notes up front with hints of raspberry on the finish.

LE GALANTIN | Bandol

Quite light in color, with medium body and acidity and subtle hints of citrus, peach, and raspberry flavors.

LES CLOS DE PAULILLES | Collioure

Tangy and bright-textured, with a focused core of cherry, citrus, and mineral flavors. Sleek on the finish.

MAS CARLOT | Costières de Nîmes

An elegant wine with moderate body and pleasing flavors that hint at cherries, rose petals, citrus, flint, and herbs. Good acidity keeps it well balanced.

MAS CORNET | Collioure

A spicy-edged wine with full body and lots of steely mineral notes. Pretty rose petal, raspberry, citrus, and cinnamon flavors as well.

MAS DE GOURGONNIER
Les Baux de Provence

A lighter style that offers bright-hued hints of citrus, mineral, raspberry, and cherry notes, finishing fresh and crisp.

MAS GRAND PLAGNIOL/MAS DES BRESSADES | Costières de Nîmes

This wine can be found under both the Mas Grand Plagniol and Mas des Bressades labels. It's imported by two different distributors who market it under separate labels. Made in a silky smooth style that blends firm acidity with supple texture and ripe lush cherry, raspberry, anise, herb, and citrus flavors. Seductive.

MOULIN DE GASSAC
Le Mazet | Vin de Pays de l'Herault

Firm, fresh, and light-textured with a pleasing array of cherry, raspberry, herb, and mineral flavors. Bright on the finish.

MOULIN DES COSTES | Bandol

Quite lemony, with steely mineral notes and a fresh, light finish.

PIERRE PLOUZEAU
Les Devants de la Bonnelière | Touraine

Very bright, with lovely cherry and raspberry aromas. On the palate it's got a distinctive herbal quality often found with Cabernet Franc grapes grown in the Loire region.

ROUTAS | Coteaux Varois

A well-balanced, light-bodied wine that serves up a fine blend of pretty citrus, cherry, herb, and mineral notes. Bright and fresh on the finish, but with a bit more roundness on the palate than similar wines from the region.

TRIENNES | Gris | Vin de Pays de Var

This one shows hints of peach and pear. It's fresh and light-textured on the palate; clean and mineral-like on the finish.

GERMANY

FRANZ WILHELM LANGGUTH
Erben Weissherbst Qualitätswein | Pfalz

This German rosé shows off a pretty peach and strawberry essence that's backed up by bright citruslike acidity and a touch of sweetness.

LINGENFELDER
Trocken Spätlese | Pfalz

A fresh and elegant style, sleek and well balanced. It's *trocken*, as the label says, which means "dry." *Spätlese* indicates the grapes were picked very ripe. Made from Pinot Noir, this may be one of Germany's finest rosés, showing hints of rose petals, raspberries, cherries, citrus, and herbs.

GREECE

AKAKIES | Amyndeon

Light and fresh on the palate, with simple herb, mineral, and citrus flavors. Clean on the finish.

DOMAINE SPIROPOULOS
Meliasto | Peloponnese

Quite light and tangy, but with a solid core of strawberry, grapefruit, and mineral flavors. Bright on the finish.

GAIA ESTATE | 14-18H | Peloponnese

The name 14-18H refers to the number of hours that the grape skins remain in contact with the juice. Bright-textured, with a strong mineral and herb component backed by cherry and citrus overtones.

ITALY

ALOIS LAGEDER
Lagrein Rosé | Alto Adige

A fresh, clean wine with moderate body and acidity and pleasing mineral, cherry, and citrus flavors at its core.

BAIA DELLE ROSE | Colline Pescaresi

A simple, straightforward style that offers cherries and herbs as its centerpiece. Moderate acidity keeps it firm on the palate.

CAMPIROSA
Cerasuolo | Montepulciano d'Abruzzo

A spicy and somewhat rich style, redolent of bright cherries, minerals, and herbs. Fresh and lemony on the finish.

CANTINA BOLZANO
"Pischl" | Alto Adige

Zippy fresh and light on the palate with a fair amount of complexity, showing hints of spice, cherry, citrus, mineral, and herb flavors. Long and refreshing on the finish.

CONTINI | Della Valle del Tirso

Moderate-bodied, this wine offers a solid cherry core highlighted by brisk lemon and mineral notes. Clean, round, and fresh on the finish.

IL MIMO | Colline Novarese | Piedmont

Rich, bold, ripe, and brimming with cherry and spice flavors. Cinnamon and cloves come to mind as well, finishing long and bright.

LA CROTTA DI VEGNERON
Vallée d'Aoste

A very light-colored pink, with a strong mineral and citrus core. Steely on the finish.

LEPORE
Cerasuolo | Montepulciano d'Abruzzo

A darker style of rosé, with rich, round cherry, herb, and citrus flavors, all balanced by moderate acidity. It's crisp and fresh on the finish, with a mineral edge.

QUATROVENTI | Rosato | Puglia
Very light textured, with subtle floral, raspberry, cherry, and citrus flavors.

REGALEALI | Sicily
A dark-hued style, with plenty of cherry, berry, anise, herb, and citrus flavors. The finish is well defined, ending with a lemony, raspberry edge.

RIVERA | Castel del Monte
A pretty wine that sports modest body, moderate acidity, and pleasing raspberry, citrus, and herb flavors.

ROSA DEL GOLFO | Salento
A smooth-textured wine, silky and fresh, that serves up a pleasing blend of raspberry, cherry, sage, lemon, and spice flavors.

SCALABRONE | Bolgheri
Bright and fresh, this rosé from the Antinori family serves up a bracing, firm blend of bing cherry, herb, mineral, and citrus flavors.

SÙLE FEBBRE | Salento
A steely, mineral style that sports hints of citrus and raspberry notes.

TRE TORRI | Carignano del Sulcis
Mild mannered, with modest hints of raspberry, citrus and herbs. The wine offers a pretty floral note on the finish.

VALENTINI
Cerasuolo | Montepulciano d'Abruzzo

An iconoclastic rosé, this wine is one of the most expensive non-sparkling rosés.

Smooth and lush, it's brimming with floral notes. With heady volatility, it is nonetheless front-loaded with complex raspberry, cherry, lemon, herb, and mineral notes. Silky textured, elegant, and long.

NEW YORK

CHANNING PERRINE
Fleur de la Terre Rosé |
North Fork of Long Island

A bright, crisp style produced in very small quantities by Long Island winemaking pioneer Larry Perrine, who made some of the first rosé ever in his region. This one, made from Merlot, is light, fresh, and easy drinking, marked by pretty strawberry, citrus, and herb flavors.

SOUTH AFRICA

GOATS DO ROAM | Paarl Valley
Bright and fresh, with zippy acidity. The wine sports a simple core of cherry and citrus flavors.

SPAIN

CONDESA DE LEGANZA | La Mancha
A bright-edged wine with a mineral/cherry core.

CUNE | Rioja
Steely clean, bright-edged, and firm-textured, this wine delivers a bracing blend of citrus, mineral, herb, and moderate strawberry flavors.

EL COTO | Rioja
With a pale salmon hue, this wine holds a bright-edged, medium-bodied array of flavors including mandarin orange, lemon, grapefruit, herbs, and spice. Light-textured on the finish.

FAUSTINO V | Rioja
Somewhat austere, with bright acidity and a citrus, cherry, and slate core.

MARQUÉS DE CÁCERES | Rioja
A truly easy-drinking, fresh, juicy wine that sports plenty of lush cherry and raspberry flavors, neatly balanced by pretty lemon, grapefruit, and mineral notes.

MARQUÉS DEL PUERTO
Rosado | Rioja

A pleasant, light-bodied wine with moderate cherry, strawberry, and mineral flavors.

MUGA | Rioja
Light pink, with good body and a pleasing core of peach and cherry flavors, balanced by a citrus/mineral edge.

OCHOA | Navarra
Fresh and lively in the nose, with hints of cherry, raspberry, and citrus aromas. Bright on the palate, with lemony fruit flavors that are supported by a steely mineral edge. Bright and clean at the end.

PAGO DE VALLEOSCURO | Benavente
A blend of Tempranillo and Prieto Picudo grapes. It's a simple, pretty wine with a cherry, raspberry core. The finish offers hints of earth and herbs.

PROTOCOLO | Castilla
Tangy and bright, yet with good body. This wine serves up a distinctive raspberry edge backed by zippy lemon and grapefruit flavors.

RENÉ BARBIER | Catalunya
Very light-bodied, simple, and fresh, with modest cherry and spice flavors.

SENORIO DE SARRIA | Navarra
A light-bodied wine with pretty cherry and mineral notes. Fresh and clean on the finish.

SUMARROCA | Penedés
Light and fresh, with a pretty core of bright cherry, thyme, sage, and citrus flavors. Easy drinking with a clean, refreshing finish that offers a mineral edge for added interest. Quite lovely.

VALDEMAR | Rioja

A bright-styled wine, with tart citrus flavors up front. They're backed by cherry and raspberry notes, finishing fresh and light.

VEGA SINDOA | Navarra

Light, fresh, and easy drinking, with hints of cherry, mineral, herbs, and citrus flavors.

WASHINGTON

SNOQUALMIE
Cirque du Rosé | Columbia Valley

A leaner style of wine that offers subtle licorice, black cherry, and herb flavors, with just a hint of spice on the finish.

STEFANO
Rose of Cabernet | Columbia Valley

A full-bodied, almost muscular style, with firm acidity and even a touch of tannic bite. Bright cherry and herbs form the flavor profile. Tangy/tart at the end.

SPARKLING WINE

AUSTRALIA

TALTARNI | Brut Taché | Victoria

Creamy-smooth, with a tangy mineral and citrus edge. It's clean and fresh, with hints of green apple and pear.

CALIFORNIA

CA'DEL SOLO FREISA (FRIZZANTE)
Monterey County

This Cal-Italianesque bubbly is on the dark side of pink. Made by Bonny Doon, it will take you back to your youth and the joys of black cherry soda, for which it's a dead ringer. But it's still got a little alcohol (4 percent), so we can feel like grown-ups as we drink. Enjoy as an aperitif.

CHANDON
Etoile Rosé | Napa/Sonoma Counties

Smooth-textured (for bubbly). The wine features tiny bubbles that help carry its blend of citrus, cherry, herb, and mineral flavors neatly along the palate. Fresh, clean, focused, and classy.

DOMAINE CARNEROS
Brut Rosé | Cuvée de la Pompadour | Carneros

Crisp and clean, with a fresh lemony edge that perks up the palate. It's followed by a hint of toast, mineral, and light strawberry flavors. Bright, yet slightly creamy on the finish.

GLORIA FERRER
Brut Rosé | Sonoma County

Light-textured and bright, this refreshing quaff displays a blend of melon, grapefruit, and strawberry flavors. Fresh and lively on the finish.

IRON HORSE | Brut Rosé | Green Valley

Fairly dark in color, this wine starts off with a bright cherry core that extends to black cherry, citrus, and herbs along the palate. It's creamy-fresh, and long on the finish.

J | Brut Rosé | Russian River Valley

A toasty, fresh style that invokes raspberry, citrus, and mineral flavors. Bright and clean on the finish.

KORBEL | Brut Rosé | California

Pale pink, with pretty apple and cherry flavors at the fore. The wine is fresh, clean, and light-textured, offering a lively, lemony, toasty finish.

LAETITIA | Brut Rosé | Arroyo Grande

A bright-edged, steely, mineral-like wine that serves up lots of citrus—lemon and grapefruit come to mind. The finish is fresh and zippy with a hint of cherries at the end.

PACIFIC ECHO
Brut Rosé | Anderson Valley

Quite fragrant, with hints of peaches,

tangerine, and wild flowers. It's creamy-rich on the palate, serving up a lovely blend of toast, green apple, citrus, pear, and grapefruit flavors. Full and rich on the finish. Really lovely.

ROEDERER ESTATE
Brut Rosé | Anderson Valley

A richly textured, plush bubbly that delivers mounds of toast, cherry, peach, pear, and floral flavors. With just enough tangy acidity to balance its body, the wine finishes long, fresh, and luxuriously.

S. ANDERSON | Rosé | Napa Valley

With its zippy acidity and solid cherry and citrus core, this is a refreshingly satisfying wine. It's got good body and a long, raspberry and mineral finish.

SCHRAMSBERG
Brut Rosé | Napa, Mendocino, Sonoma

Sleek and elegant, with a toasty, spice aroma up front. Bright cherry, citrus, mineral, and herb flavors blend seamlessly here. The bubbles comport themselves with finesse and elegance, finishing fresh at the end.

SJOEBLOM WINERY
Chauvignon Crystal | Napa Valley

Made from Cabernet rather than Pinot Noir, this pink bubbly is bright and fresh tasting, with pretty citrus, raspberry, cherry, toast, and herb flavors at the fore. Clean and zippy on the finish, it's full and round yet light and complex. The wine shows that fine bubbly can be made outside its normal varietal parameters.

FRANCE

BOLLINGER
Grande Année | Champagne

This is a bubbly that's lush and richly textured. It sports complex flavors of hazelnuts, melon, citrus, herbs, violets, and raspberries. Like most high-end Champagne, the wine benefits from extended bottle age before release, which gives it greater complexity.

CHAMPAGNE DEUTZ
Rosé Brut | Champagne

Richly textured, round and full on the palate, with fresh, lively raspberry and cherry flavors at its core. This vintage-dated wine serves up bright citrus and mineral notes for added interest, and is framed with a toasty edge.

CHARLES HEIDSIECK
Brut Rosé | Champagne

An exceedingly toasty, rich style that sports lots of earth and nut tones, backed by hints of pear and citrus flavors. Full-bodied and lush.

FRÉDÉRIC LORNET
Crémant du Jura | Brut Jura

In the language of bubbly, *crémant* usually means the wine is fairly sweet. This one's not; and it's not from Champagne either. It's from the Jura region, farther south. The sparkler is, nonetheless, richly textured and only very slightly "off dry." Creamy-smooth on the finish, it's got a charming cherry and herb core that leaves the palate fresh and lively.

G.H. MUMM & CO.
Brut-Rosé | Champagne

Fresh, bright, and brimming with citrus, raspberry, toast, herb, spice, and mineral flavors. This is a lovely, classy, and refreshing bubbly.

GOSSET | Grand Rosé Brut | Champagne

With hints at first of raspberry, spice, and toast aromas, the wine follows up with green apple, lemon, mineral, herb, and grapefruit flavors. Bright and clean on the finish.

HENRIOT
Rosé Millésime Brut | Champagne

An elegant sparkler, with moderate body and a fresh, silky texture. The flavors range from strawberry and apple to citrus, pear, and herbs. Flinty and clean on the finish. This winery's got some staying power: the bottle foil says "founded in 1808."

KRUG | Rosé | Champagne

If it's possible to describe fine Champagne as "big," this one fits the bill. Full-bodied and richly textured, Krug rosé comes from one of France's most venerable houses. It's barely pink, but rather a deep, golden color. Brimming with honey, toast, pear, citrus, hazelnut, and spice flavors, this lush sparkler is a blueprint for pure hedonism on the palate. Like many of the best bubblies, it's not cheap. But it is thoroughly satisfying.

LANSON | Rosé | Champagne

A toasty style of bubbly, with a broad range of flavors that speak of peach, pear, green apple, spice, and citrus flavors. Refreshing but nonetheless full-bodied.

LAURENT PERRIER
Cuvée Rosé Brut | Champagne

A well-balanced wine that offers a fairly rich texture, good weight on the palate, and a charming cherry, herb, and citrus quality. Fresh and lively, it ends with a toasty edge. Also comes in a kosher version that is equally appealing.

LAURENT PERRIER
Grand Siècle | Alexandra Rosé | Champagne

Fresh and light, like a fine bubbly should be. This wine is a bit frisky, with bright acidity and tangy-fresh lemon and toast flavors.

LOUIS ROEDERER
Cristal | Champagne Brut Rosé | Champagne

Richly textured, creamy, and lush, this top-of-the-line bubbly is more golden than rosé. It's touched with hazelnut, honey, toast, spice, mandarin orange, grapefruit, and bright-edged lemon flavors. Long and fresh on the finish; very elegant.

MOËT & CHANDON
Cuvée Dom Pérignon | Rosé | Champagne

A fine-tuned top-of-the-line wine that serves up plenty of finesse. Usually about ten years old upon release, with focused, bright-edged flavors redolent of raspberry, cherry, grapefruit, lemon, toast, and herbs. Fresh yet long on the finish.

MOËT & CHANDON
Millésime Rosé | Champagne

A light-hued pink bubbly with plenty of elegance and finesse, sporting flavors redolent of cherry, raspberry, peach, and citrus flavors, all framed in toasty, complex nuance.

NICOLAS FEUILLATTE
Brut Premier Cru Rosé | Champagne

A bright, steely style of wine that shows mineral and citrus qualities on the sparkling finish.

NICOLAS FEUILLATE
Cuvée Palmes d'Or | Rosé-Brut | Champagne

A complex, top-of-the-line wine with hints of raspberry, blackberry, minerals, spice, and herbs. Focused and elegant, long and fresh to the end.

PAUL GOERG | Brut Rosé | Champagne

This was tasted out of a privately cellared magnum; probably about ten years old and really delicious. Smooth, creamy, and complex, with hints of floral notes, citrus, peach, honey, toast, and hazelnuts. Lush.

PERRIER JOUËT
Blason Rosé | Champagne

Fine-textured and sleekly elegant, with a good balance of citrus, herb, lemon, and raspberry flavors. The finish is bright and toasty.

PERRIER JOUËT
Fleur de Champagne | Rosé | Champagne

Fresh and lively, with a pretty raspberry and citrus core. Light on the finish. This one's got the famous art deco flowers painted on the bottle.

PIPER-HEIDSIECK
Brut Rosé | Champagne

Crisp, yet richly textured, with toasty aromas hinting of fresh baked bread. The flavors range from lemon to grapefruit, with subtle cherry and mineral notes on the finish.

POMMERY | Brut Rosé | Champagne

A smooth, elegant non-vintage sparkler that sounds notes of apricot, citrus, herb, and raspberry. Bright and toasty, fresh and clean on the finish.

RENÉ GEOFFROY
Brut Rosé de Saignée | Champagne | Cumieres

A broad-shouldered bubbly, with plush cherry, herb, lemon, and toast flavors. It's full-bodied and richly textured, focused, and elegant. Quite pink in color.

TAITTINGER
Comtes de Champagne | Brut Rosé | Champagne

A very toasty wine, backed by modest raspberry and herb flavors. Fairly broad on the palate, with a tangy finish.

VEUVE CLICQUOT PONSARDIN
La Grande Dame | Brut Rosé | Champagne

This top-of-the-line pink sparkler from Veuve Clicquot is elegant and smooth-textured. The bubbles are small and carry flavors redolent of strawberry, toast, dough, minerals, black cherry, peach, and herbs deftly across the palate. Fresh and long on the finish.

VEUVE CLICQUOT PONSARDIN
Rosé | Champagne

Crisp and elegant, with pretty toast, citrus, apple, raspberry, pear, melon, spice, and mineral flavors. Fresh, clean, and long on the finish, this is a vintage-dated wine.

VIN DE BUGEY
Cerdon | Méthode Ancestrale | Demi-Sec

Quite pink, with a well-defined cherry/raspberry core that's tempered by good acidity and tiny bubbles. It offers a subtle touch of sweetness on the finish. A fine aperitif.

ITALY

BARTOLOMEO ROSATO
Veneto Rosato | Frizzante

Fresh and bright on the palate, this *frizzante* has only a hint of sweetness, making it suitable for both an aperitif and dinner. Offering cherry, herb, and citrus notes, it's light and lively to the end.

BELLAVISTA
Gran Cuvée | Brut Rosé | Franciacorta

A steely dry bubbly, with vigorous lemon and herb flavors that dominate. Hints of toast and raspberries round it off.

CONTADI CASTALDI | Franciacorta

Richly textured, full, and fresh on the palate, with seductive toast, spice, cherry, apple, ginger, lemon, and mineral flavors. This is a very fine vintage-dated Italian bubbly.

ELIO PERRONE
Bigaro | Moscato d'Asti

Only slightly fizzy with charming hints of ginger, raspberry, lemon, and spice. Sweet, yet elegant, and well balanced. A fine palate teaser for before dinner.

ROTARI
Blanc de Noir | Brut Rosé | Trento

Quite bright and firm with zippy citrus and herb notes. Sleek and light on the finish. Just barely pink.

VITICOLTORI DELL'ACQUESE
Frizzante | Brachetto d'Acqui

A dark-hued pink that's almost red, this slightly sparkling, low-alcohol (about 6 percent) wine makes a lovely aperitif or after-dinner drink. It's sweet, yet refreshing, with bright cherry and spice flavors at the fore.

SPAIN

CRISTALINO | Rosé Brut

A well-structured bubbly with crisp citrus, herb, and bitter cherry flavors. On the finish, it's fairly long, sleek, and bright.

FREIXENET | Cava Brut de Noirs

Bright and fresh, with a cherry and lemon core that's clean on the palate. It's got a hint of mineral and herb on the finish, which adds interest.

MARQUÉS DE MONISTROL
Cava Reserva | Selección Especial

A lemony bright blend that serves up hints of cherry, raspberry, and herbs, finishing with moderate length.

PARXET | Cava | Pinot Noir Brut

Starts off with toasty, yeasty notes in the nose. On the palate, it's got a strong herbal component that remains throughout the finish, backed by hints of raspberry.

PARXET | Cuvée Dessert | Pinot Noir

As its name implies, this bubbly is somewhat sweet, although not overpoweringly so. It's balanced with hints of ginger and herbs and finishes with a lemony lift.

TORRE ORIA | Demi Sec

A spicy, sparkling blend of cherry and raspberry flavors that finishes with a pretty cinnamon edge. Slightly sweet, it makes a fine aperitif.

INDEX

TABLE OF EQUIVALENTS

LIQUID/DRY MEASURES

U.S.	METRIC	U.S.	METRIC
1/4 teaspoon	1.25 milliliters	1 cup	240 milliliters
1/2 teaspoon	2.5 milliliters	1 pint (2 cups)	480 milliliters
1 teaspoon	5 milliliters	1 quart (4 cups, 32 ounces)	960 milliliters
1 tablespoon (3 teaspoons)	15 milliliters	1 gallon (4 quarts)	3.84 liters
1 fluid ounce (2 tablespoons)	30 milliliters	1 ounce (by weight)	28 grams
1/4 cup	60 milliliters	1 pound	454 grams
1/3 cup	80 milliliters	2.2 pounds	1 kilogram
1/2 cup	120 milliliters		

LENGTH

U.S.	METRIC
1/8 inch	3 millimeters
1/4 inch	6 millimeters
1/2 inch	12 millimeters
1 inch	2.5 centimeters

The exact equivalents in the tables have been rounded for convenience.

OVEN TEMPERATURE

FAHRENHEIT	CELSIUS	GAS
250	120	1/2
275	140	1
300	150	2
325	160	3
350	180	4
375	190	5
400	200	6
425	220	7
450	230	8
475	240	9
500	260	10